Buckskins, Blades & Biscuits

Buckskins, Blades & Biscuits

Allen Kent Johnston
Text and Drawings

hancock

house

ISBN 0-88839-363-6
Copyright © 1995 Allen Johnston

Cataloging in Publication Data
Johnston, Allen, 1931-1993
Buckskins, blades, and biscuits

ISBN 0-88839-363-6

1. Cookery, American—History. 2. Frontier and pioneer
life. 3. Leatherwork. I. Title.
TX703.J66 1995   641.5973   C95-910150-0

Printed in Hong Kong-Jade Productions

Copy edit: Colin Lamont
Production: Myron Shutty, Lorna Brown, and Jeffrey Stilz

Cover Photo: Lloyd Gillis. Back row: John Roberts, Marvin Brandt, Bill Perry,
Lewis Iselin, Jim Lackey, Billy Hibbs, and Bob Neal. Front row: Lloyd Gillis,
Little Wayne, Greg Weidman, Rhonda Neal, Fred McNeil, Mike Pence, John
Christoff, and Roger Fowler.

Published simultaneously in Canada and the United States by

HANCOCK HOUSE PUBLISHERS LTD.
19313 Zero Avenue, Surrey, B.C. V4P 1M7
(604) 538-1114   Fax (604) 538-2262

HANCOCK HOUSE PUBLISHERS
1431 Harrison Avenue, Blaine, WA 98230-5005
(604) 538-1114   Fax (604) 538-2262

Contents

The Red River Renegades

A fine group of people—men, women, and youngsters of Wichita Falls and vicinity, Texas and Oklahoma—drawn together by the common interest and enjoyment of black powder shooting in the old tradition. Without their enthusiasm and encouragement, this collection of accouterments and designs might never have been compiled.

The Great American Frontier

The vast uninhabited and beautiful country of the land west of the Mississippi River fired the imagination of all men. The common desire of the average man of the middle 1700s and early 1800s, whether he would admit it or not, was to move into and become part of the new land. There were those who gave up everything and moved blindly into the expanding frontier. Others brought goods and services with them to establish themselves as blacksmith, doctor, cooper, merchant, cobbler, and all other lines of endeavor. The more hardy moved out beyond the inhabited frontier settlements. Exploration and exploitation was a common drive and brought honest and dishonest men alike. The new land was a land of plenty with tens of thousands of square miles of timber, millions of acres of lush grasslands, fish, fowl, and game enough to fill the larder forever.

The times were turbulent, war with France then with England stirred the adventurous to fight for causes they may or may not have understood. Young men got caught up in the excitement and found that they had to have excitement and adventure to be able to continue life. Thomas Jefferson sent Lewis and Clark and Lieutenant Pike to explore and report on new land, new routes, and resources. Hunters, trappers, and traders brought back stories of beauty, adventure, and riches to be gleaned from the broad land.

Life in the infant United States was hard and, by modern standards, primitive. Self-reliance was the foundation upon which most of the families were built. There were needs which were met in the home, spinning yarn to weave cloth for making clothing, tanning hides for shoes and harnesses, and, in the barns and sheds, bits and pieces of iron were heated and forged to make a multitude of items required for everyday living and working. These were the homes and farms of the common man. Every child was introduced to the industry of everyday living. Hunting and trapping brought food and hides into the home. Farming and gardening provided more needs. The excess items of the industry went to neighbors in trade for other needs. Money was scarce, barter was the game of life. Living was scarcely more than camping in a permanent shelter. Water had to be carried from the nearest stream or hand dug well. Wood had to be cut and brought in for fuel. Sanitation was an outhouse, at best. Corn shucks, leaves, moss, boughs, and anything else which was soft as well as insulating made a mattress to make nights more bearable.

The frontiersman sprung from this environment. Adaptation to the wilderness was much simpler than it would be for the modern American. Much of the mode of living off of the land and adapting to the environment was the gift of the American Indian. It was the Indian and his ways that got the colonists through the first few winters. Technology from the Old World brought guns, iron and steel tools and implements, cloth, and other items which made the simple life more bearable. Medicine in the frontier was as crude as if none existed. A simple rule of life was that a person was born, he lived, and he died. There was no emergency in the wilderness. Death was a constant companion to the frontiersman and Indian alike.

Yet, the call of the wilderness was strong. Answering the call were men and women from all walks of life, from all races and creeds. There were many who could read and write and of those, some wrote letters and journals which have been preserved for accurate historical records. Most of the hunters, trappers, and traders left no record of their own, so the full story of the adventures and hardships of the mountain man or plainsman is unknown.

The Rocky Mountains are unchanged from what they were 200 years ago. Some of the timber has been cut away, and some has been burned off, but traces of the early mountain men still remain. Old cabins, long since rotted down to the ground, can still be found in hidden and well protected places. Poking around in the ruins produces many treasures from the bygone eras. The treasures may be no more than an old ax head, a rusted tin cup, a fragment of pottery from a vessel traded from the Indians, a lead ball, a broken flint, or the bent jaw of a steel trap.

The tracks of modern civilization crisscross the wilderness now: logging roads, power transmission lines, highways and bridges, and overhead the contrail of a high flying jet airplane. The tracks are marks of progress and have a right to be there, as much a right as the pottery shards and flint chips of an ancient Indian village or the tumbled down ruins of the pilgrim's cabin. All of these things mark the passage of man through the environment.

Greed of men, both past and present, has raped the land, but ignorance of the ways of nature has done more damage than mere desire for wealth. The early American, the Indian, took only what he needed for his daily life, as did the wolf, the bear, or even the field mouse. The demands of the civilized world for hides, fur, lumber, minerals, grazing land, water, and other resources precipitated a drain on the natural wealth of this great land of ours. People are realizing the wrongs brought about by so many for so long and movements are now underway to try to salvage what can be saved. Nostalgia prompts men and women to pursue the past in one way or another.

The growth rate of the black powder fraternity has been phenomenal. The rank and file is comprised of people from all walks of life tied together by a common thread, black gunpowder and the things that go with it. Not all of the fraternity are dyed-in-the-wool shooters, many are coming to the ranges to try their hand at shooting for the first time with a desire to learn and participate. If a poll were taken of the people buying muzzle loading arms, and if they were honest with their answers, we would find a variety of reasons for their purchase:

"I don't know, but I've always wanted one," or "I've always admired the makers of early American history and this brings me closer to the scenes of Lexington or Concord," or "I've shot everything from .22 to 12 gauge and this looks like fun," or even "I enjoy the pageantry."

I believe the real reason lies in an individual's desire to escape the hurry-hurry of today's frantic pace. We live in a world of hurry, in business, transportation, communication, and even entertainment. Electronic computers further accelerate the pace as each

11

business tries to get the jump on its competition. Television and motion picture entertainment reflect the pace as well. A story of sixty or ninety minutes may cover the time frame of a full day, a week, or even years and involve high speed chases and thrill-a-minute action. Almost everything we do today is geared to race the clock. I believe that the "something" that draws people to the past is the leisurely pace enjoyed so long ago.

Today, it is still easy to return to such a setting. All you need to do is locate the nearest Black Powder shoot and make it a priority to be there. As you pass through the range gate you will find that you have crossed the threshold of times past. Look around! You can see individuals dressed as Confederate cavalry officers, Union soldiers, mountain men, plainsmen, and some dressed as frontier folk. In fact, entire families can be seen dressed in buckskins and hand made clothing of coarse and colorful materials. Don't feel out of place with your baseball cap and sneakers because that shooter on the line in T-shirt and tennis shoes is doing his thing too. Besides, these costumes are not the result of a trip to the local man's or woman's shop for an outfit. These clothes are the fruits of many weeks of planning, days of working and sewing, weeks of locating or waiting for materials, and untold hours of research in the library. Some of these outfits represent a year or more of patience and development. Remember, you are back in a period where time means nothing and the clock is the sun. The times of the day are sunup, high noon, sundown, and night, where spring and fall are the big events of the year.

As you look back behind the range you see tepees, lean-tos, and other primitive shelters where these people camp while attending the weekend shoot. There are traders with a multitude of items ranging from breads to gun barrels, buckskins to Hudson Bay blankets, and handmade gimcracks of every description. Off to one side, a group is throwing tomahawks at a mark on a stump, and elsewhere some others are throwing knives at a wooden backstop. Everyone is doing his own thing, together.

Stroll down the barrier back of the firing line and look at the array of muzzleloaders being used for the shooting matches. The guns range from homemade, through kit and store shelf models, to custom made rifles from questionable quality. There are even shooting antiques that made it through the rigors of westward expansion.

The people are friendly; they have time to be. Conversations are going on everywhere. No, they are not talking jobs, politics, insurance, or religion. They are talking about carving bone, polishing steel, stitching and lacing buckskin, periods in history, the shape of a blade, or the width of a front sight. The world outside of the range fence has been forgotten for the day. However, they all share one regret, that along about sundown they will have to get into their individual vehicles and return to the twentieth century.

Most of the people you meet at the range have another refuge from frenzy at home. It may be a corner in the living room or a workbench in the garage. There they clean their guns, sharpen a patch knife, work on some new project, or read a historical novel. They have found the secret of a more leisurely leisure, a way to slow down and enjoy life their way. I have been enjoying life this way for years. Whenever the pressures of today's frantic pace begin to tell on my nervous system, I know it is time to retreat to the high country of Colorado, Wyoming, or Montana during the 1820s. I imagine I'm confined to a snowed-in trapper's cabin, then, I can set to work on a new spring outfit of beaded buckskins, a carved powder horn, or a new knife sheath.

Planning for these projects has been equally enjoyable. A sketch pad and pencil go with me everywhere. When there is an occasion to visit a museum, I make the time. If there is some eye-catching item of clothing or equipment on display, it is recorded as a sketch with details noted. Then, during odd moments, it is redone into a finished drawing. Most of the drawings never go any farther than the sketchbook. Planning is not intended to reproduce or counterfeit a particular item from a historical collection, but to record style, materials, and workmanship of the period. From these sketches, I select what is appealing to me and combine them into an item of period authenticity. I did not invent the powder horn or knife sheath, but I am rediscovering them.

So many of the rediscovered items transcend time lines of history that it becomes evident that people of any particular period were doing the same thing. They found some item that was necessary or useful and either reproduced or adapted it to their needs.

These people lived at a time when supply was far short of demand and nothing was wasted, not even ideas. Today, with mass production, ready supply, and designed obsolescence, the dump grounds and land fills are full of discarded but useable items. I have dug in old dumps near collapsed cabins, ruins of a stagecoach relay station, forts, and old town sites and found comparatively little. There were the usual buttons, coins, shoe nails, patent medicine bottles, fragments of broken pottery and china, but very few metal items. Metals were precious and the people salvaged every useful piece whether it was steel or pewter. Archaeologists of the future will find a bonanza of items in our land fills and will name this era "The Era of Waste." How right they will be!

This book has been put together as a book of accouterments or accessories to the historical costume, shooting equipment, and personal items for the rendezvous trade or blanket shoot. This book is not a catalog, there is no merchandise to sell. Rather, I want to share some ideas, experiences, and hours of pleasure-filled relaxation with you. The time frame of this collection of accouterments is generally the century-and-a-half from 1700 to 1850.

When using this book, try to think and be like the hunter, trapper, or pioneer. Play the role to its fullest. Make your own tools. Do as much as possible by hand and adapt crude or raw materials to your projects. Be aware of the trials and hardships faced by the people of the times. By making an item of wood, horn, bone, or hide, you are actually recreating a moment in the history of your nation. The finished product, not only reflects your labors and pride, but becomes a small monument to the people who carved this country out of wilderness, your forbearers and mine.

Bags and Pouches

Pouches, bags, purses, pokes, and sacks by any and all names date back to the dawn of civilization. These containers made it possible for people of the world to carry their belongings, needs, treasures, and impediments as they moved from place to place. Garments of the people down through the ages covered nakedness without much regard to pockets. Bags were made of skins, leathers, cloth, straw, reeds; in fact, anything that could be formed into serviceable containers. Every manner of carry has been used by men and women through time.

Early European hunters and soldiers carried shoulder bags long before the advent of the firearm. Their pouches probably carried a sling and a few well chosen rocks, arrow points, cross-bolts, as well as odds and ends of personal comforts. It was natural that, with the advent of the long Pennsylvanian rifle, a shoulder pouch would be well established as a piece of wilderness equipment. We can only speculate as to how, when, and where the term "possible" came to be associated with the shoulder pouch.

Nearly every shooter who has been in the black powder shooting game for six months or more has a possible bag. Some shooters own several and are still looking for the "right" bag. Every one of us eyes the pouches carried by other shooters at the range looking for features to be included in the "ultimate" possible bag of our dreams. There are several sources of bags and pouches which include some attractive and serviceable leather purses made in Mexico. Various leather and do-it-yourself hobby centers carry a wide selection of precut purse kits. There are also many styles and qualities of hand-made possible bags sold by traders at various club shoots. Possible bags are not inexpensive, and you can invest quite a bit of money in bags before you are satisfied, if ever.

BAGS AND POUCHES

POSSIBLE BAGS

©ALLEN K. JOHNSTON   WICHITA FALLS, TEXAS   1979

PLATE 1

16

Selecting the right bag requires many considerations, the first being what is to be carried in the bag. Every book, guide, and magazine article dealing with front-end-loading merely mention the possible bag only to enlighten the novice black powder shooter as to its usual contents. The pouch is often referred to as a shooting kit, survival kit, bag of tricks, etc., etc. All of these ideas and opinions are correct but there are still other uses not yet redis- covered. Basically, the possible bag carried all that was necessary to keep the long rifle or shotgun firing. This list includes: balls, patches, flints, caps, worm, jag, vent pick, flint knapper, screw- driver, nipple wrench, powder measure, prepared charges, ad infi- nitum. To this list the wilderness pilgrim adds flint and steel, a pair of socks, some charqui (jerky), and anything else he had room for to make the wilderness more endurable. There were no hard and fast rules governing the use of the pouch, so the man in the woods back then did as he pleased, and the same rules apply today. If you are going to the range, take what you will need for the day. If you are going into some river bottom to shoot squirrels, add whatever you anticipate you will want to make the hunt a success. It's your bag and you're stuck with the contents, right or wrong.

The above concept is, then, one criterion for selecting the right bag to fill your needs. Assemble the basic equipment that will be needed for shooting and lay it out on a table. Try to take into account any possible need or problem that may arise. For example, you may need a spare nipple or a little dab of grease. When you are satisfied with the inventory, stack the gear together to see how much room it will take up. Then see if anything can be carried in smaller containers to reduce the load volume. Now, you are ready to determine the size and style of pouch you will need. I have found that the best method is to make some mock-up bags out of paper and glue. Make several models and include pockets and dividers you feel you will need. Once the ideal setup has been worked out, it can be measured and turned into a pattern, or an appropriate sized bag kit can be selected.

The second consideration, whether you start from scratch or assemble a kit, is the design or pattern. It should be selected according to costume and period of history if you are a history buff, or according to need and utility if you want to go modern but

17

POSSIBLE BAGS

© ALLEN K. JOHNSTON   WICHITA FALLS, TEXAS   1979

PLATE 2

shoot black powder. Authenticity of costume depends on materials used in the making of the possible bag, the assembly of the components, and the adornment of the finished product. Natural materials such as leather, rawhide, and fur along with quasi-natural materials of wool blanket fabric and cotton canvas are used in the making of hunting pouches. I have seen several very attractive and authentic bags made with crocheted flaxen yarn which has been trimmed and reinforced with leather. Buckskin or leather lacing, or hand stitching with heavy, waxed linen thread or sinew were the only means of assembling the shoulder bags, as the sewing machine did not make its debut in the leather industry until 1857. Careful, well-spaced saddle stitching by hand is almost indistinguishable from machine stitching.

Adornment of the possible bag is another consideration and may take many forms. Designs of leather bags can be carved, burned, or painted to suit the individual. Carving leather, as we see it today, was not generally known on the frontier. The art of carving, beveling, shading, camouflage, background, etc., were trade secrets belonging to Old World craftsmen. Ornamental leather work was expensive, affordable only by royalty and nobility. Carved designs of the 1700s were commonly scenes of the hunt, nude maidens frolicking in the woods, or romantic scenes of battle. Suitable leather for carving was scarce and very expensive, so little of it was wasted on scroll work. Carvings on the frontiersman's possible bag were restricted to simple knife cuts through the slick, hair side surface of the leather. The cuts were filled with dye or a mixture of grease and soot to bring out the designs. Generally, the carvings were simple scrolls and initials, sometimes patriotic and religious scenes or designs were used. Other ornamentations commonly used were fur strips, fringe, beaded Indian designs, hex symbols, and good luck charms.

The pouches carried by the uniformed Continental soldier were usually small, black, slick leather box-shaped containers for gun equipment and cartridges. It was an issue item and had no individuality. The volunteer soldier, however, carried any bag he happened to own. These troops were from the villages, frontier, and wilderness. The term of enlistment for the volunteer was too short to justify the issue of equipment, and it is not too unlikely that they

BELT POUCHES

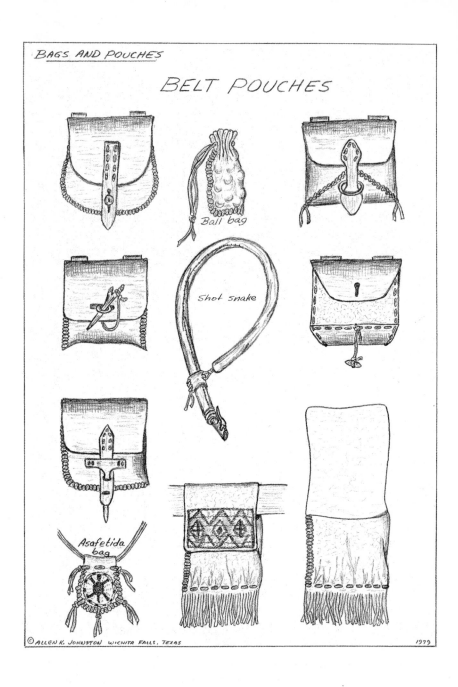

Ball bag

Shot snake

Asafetida bag

© ALLEN K. JOHNSTON WICHITA FALLS, TEXAS   1979

PLATE 3

would have refused to use issue gear. Volunteer riflemen, answering the call to colors, have always been an independent lot.

The frontiersman lived on the edge of civilization where he was close to the wilderness and also close to sources of goods from the mills of the east. He was in the position of being able to supplement his farming or craft with the harvest of the forest. He had a choice of leathers with which to make necessities for his farm and family. It was not uncommon for the frontiersman to trade hides for leather on a several for one basis. The best leather available at the time was the oil-tanned harness leather from which he made everything from shoes to door hinges. For the costume of the frontiersman, a possible bag made of a russet harness leather would be about as authentic as a man could get.

Farther from the frontier was the plainsman. He got into civilization occasionally, but spent most of his life on the prairie having to make do with what he was able to provide for himself. The materials available to the plainsman were leathers and rawhide which he or the Indians made from the skins of the plains antelope and buffalo, or from deer found in draws and wooded valleys of rivers and streams. Occasionally, the plainsman would bring hides back to civilization and trade them for supplies then return to the prairie. Bags made of harness leather would be authentic for him as would pouches of rawhide, buckskin, and poorly tanned leather. Modern leather available for making possible bags include a heavy cowhide split, for the lower grade of leather available to the plainsman; as well as harness leather, rawhide, or cow or deer hide tanned with the hair on.

Possible bags for the mountain man becomes a wide open field. The mountain man probably left civilization with the quality pouch made of heavy oil-tanned harness leather. By the end of the year, the bag bore little resemblance to the original. Every time it needed to be patched or repaired, he used whatever he had at hand to do the job. A long split was laced together with a piece of buckskin. The holes he cut in the flap to get tough leather to make new soles for his boots, were patched with elk hide. The shoulder strap he used to make a belt for his pants was replaced with plaited buckskin. And so it went, until his bag was a patchwork of furs and hides, but it still held what he needed to carry with him. Eventu-

© ALLEN K. JOHNSTON WICHITA FALLS, TEXAS   1979

PLATE 4

DESIGNS OF COLONIAL TIMES

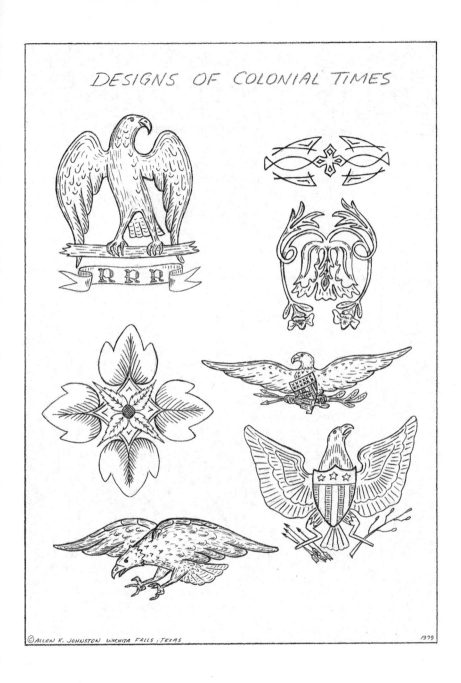

1979

PLATE 5

23

ally, the mountain man returned to civilization to sell his furs and re-outfit for his next sojourn. He outfitted in cotton or wool clothing, new boots and socks, and probably, a new harness-leather possible bag. It is reasonable to assume that he burned or buried his old buckskins but still carried or wore some favorite items or a bear claw necklace that he won in a close encounter with the original owner.

Small purses and pouches hanging from the belt or waist band and from strings around the neck are accessory items that lend a touch of authenticity to the historic costume. Tobacco and pipe bags were carried around the neck to prevent breaking the frail clay pipes. Purses held what few coins, trade beads, and other valuables the pilgrim possessed. Remember, pockets in authentic buckskin and canvas trousers are few so that the small bags will be useful to the costume as well as ornamental. Accessory pouches can be left plain or decorated with colorful designs. A splash of color adds to the costume. Stay with the period and use Indian designs, luck symbols, and hex signs done in bead or paint. The size of the small bag is a matter of personal preference. It is always enjoyable to be able to pull some item out of a belt pouch that fits the discussion or creates interest. One pouch of interest is the seamless pouch made from the rawhide or tanned scrotum of a deer or an elk. This is guaranteed to start a conversation back of the firing line.

Pistol Holsters

The pistols of the 1700 to 1850 era were poor weapons at their best. They were too big and awkward to carry comfortably and their range and accuracy was very limited. True, it was another shot at point-blank range after a rifle had expended its ball. Also, when swung enthusiastically, the pistol made a fair club. Still, carrying the thing posed problems. The pistol could be carried in a holster or bag slung from the pommel of the saddle without difficulty. The man on foot carried it the best he could if he felt the pistol was worth the weight and trouble.

We are accustomed to seeing the neat, flowing lines of holsters made for modern weapons. Making a holster for a flintlock pistol is complicated by the graceful profile of the pistol being drastically broken by the cock and steel. The lines of a holster made for the weapon must be broken to accommodate this feature. Caplock pistols pose a similar problem, although the cock does not rise quite as high above the barrel.

Three designs for pistol holsters with covers are illustrated in Plate 6. This may give you a point of departure for designing and making a holster to go with your historic costume. Use the appropriate materials for making your design and the finished product will be just as authentic as any antique. The mountain men or plainsmen did the same thing, if it needed a cover....they covered it.

The top pattern illustrated is made from soft, pliable leather. Wool blanket material would also be an excellent choice for making this holster. Notice the line of ties on the flap. They hold the main crease so that the flap will always fold correctly. The bangles hanging from the flap serve as weights to close the cover and hold it closed while in the carrying position. A heavy brass button,

PISTOL HOLSTERS

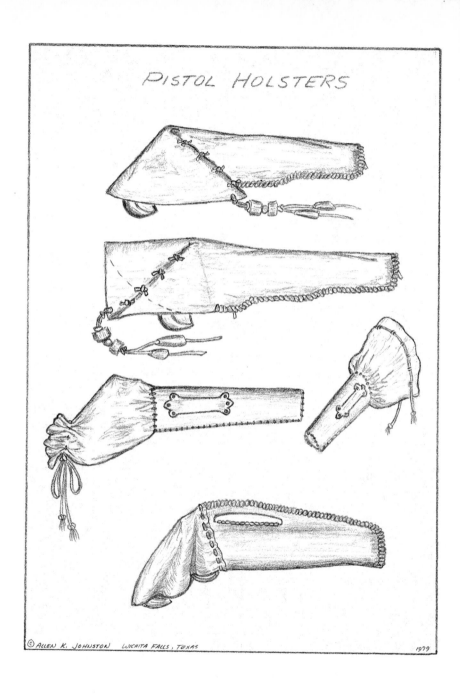

© ALLEN K. JOHNSTON   WICHITA FALLS, TEXAS   1979

PLATE 6

26

charm, or coin stitched to the flap would provide weight if the bangles are undesirable. A large beaded pattern sewn to the flap would serve as a weight and add a splash of color to the holster. Fringe, leather strings, and fur strips, should be added to suit your decorating taste.

The center pattern is made with a stiff, heavy leather body and a soft pliable material for the cover. A rich red or royal purple velvet cover makes a beautiful holster and adds much color to a suit of skins. This makes an authentic holster dating back to the French-Canadian trappers and traders of the 1700s. If you choose this elegant style, don't forget to use a gold or silver drawstring to close the velvet cover. A belt loop should be placed on both sides of the leather body to add to the utility of the holster so it can be worn in a variety of ways.

The bottom pattern uses a simple buckskin or blanket drape to cover the lock. The body is made of thick, heavy leather or rawhide in a pattern similar to a knife sheath. As the illustration is drawn, the leather body stops at the trigger guard. An alternate design can be made by extending the body beyond the trigger guard, then turning a lip upward to form a cup to hold the guard. The pistol will have to be lifted slightly to disengage the trigger guard from the holster before drawing the arm.

Rifle Covers

The long flintlock rifle was a miserable, cantankerous, fragile, expensive, poor excuse for a weapon; but it was the best in the world in its time. There were so many shortcomings in flintlock muskets and rifles that Ben Franklin proposed that the Continental army be armed with bows and arrows. He contended that the longbow possessed fair range and accuracy, was silent, gave no smoke to betray position, and several arrows could be released in the time the flintlock weapon could be fired, reloaded, and primed for a second shot. A wounded man could fight with a lead ball under his hide while the psychology of a shaft protruding from even a minor wound would put him out of action. Our Continental Congress voted to continue the use of firearms rather than to adopt the longbow.

The wilderness pilgrim was aware of the shortcomings of his rifle and did everything he could to pamper it. When the weather was miserable, his rifle was given shelter before he considered himself. At night, he bedded down with his gun resting beside him under the blanket using his body heat to help drive away moisture. The dependability of the long rifle was directly proportional to the amount of tender loving care it was given. The rifleman made a cover for his weapon to shed water when it rained, turn dust when the trail was dry, and act as a pad to protect the piece from unintentional bumps and falls.

Gun covers were made of leather and cloth, open at the butt end and stitched or laced from butt to muzzle. The case was made weather resistant by working enough animal tallow into the material to make it shed water in a rainstorm but sparingly enough to prevent condensation. Fur skin was excellent case material because the hair could be lightly greased to turn water and the leather

RIFLE COVERS

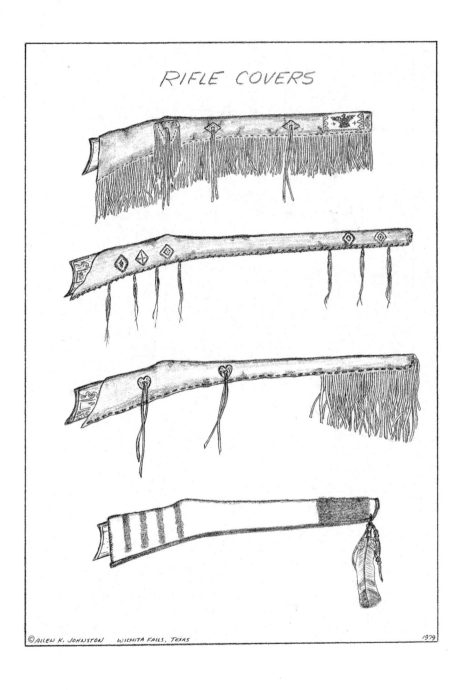

©ALLEN K. JOHNSTON   WICHITA FALLS, TEXAS   1979

PLATE 7

29

could still breathe. Mountain men made their gun covers from whatever was available to them. Because of the importance of the gun and the amount of care it was given, the pilgrim developed an attachment to his weapon not unlike a love affair. He adorned his rifle case with bangles and beaded or painted designs. Bangles, many times, reflected the performance of the rifle. A collection of bear teeth, each one representing a dead bear, or strings of hair from a scalp lock, or other scorecards. Beaded designs, common to the tribe of Indians the plainsman lived among, often served to ward off evil spirits as well as other Indians. Most of the time ornamentation served no purpose other than decoration for the pioneer's loved and respected companion, his rifle.

Powder Horns and Flasks

The powder horn was a common item carried by the early pioneer. Generally, it was common by the fact that a powder receptacle was required to keep the long rifle or musket firing. Actually, each powder horn was unique. The mountain man, soldier, frontiersman, and plainsman each bestowed a labor of love and his finest work as he carved and decorated his powder horn. It was not a love of the item itself, but it was usually his expression of his desires, sentiments, and patriotism.

Carefully inscribed powder horns found in museums and private collections expressed the individuality of the owner. Horns were inscribed with names of friends and comrades, as well as poems, prayers, and slogans. Patriotic and religious ornamentation were shared with more nostalgic scenes such as the landscape of the family home or some scene inspired by a memorable hunt. Many horns were carved with maps which depicted routes of march and locations of battles fought, as well as directions to faraway places that the owner may, or may not, have explored.

Today, as we re-create our favorite periods of history, we can express our own individuality. A one-of-a-kind powder horn or flask can be had for a few dollars worth of materials and several hours of simple hand work. Remember, there were no standards of design or construction in 1700. Stay with natural materials and hand work and the finished product will pass any purist's scrutiny.

The authentic early American powder horn represented a product of the farm or the buffalo prairie. The frontiersman or mountain man probably had a harder time obtaining a satisfactory horn than we have today. Horns suitable for making powder receptacles were not widely distributed and other materials often had to be substituted. Powder containers were made from wood, antler, rawhide,

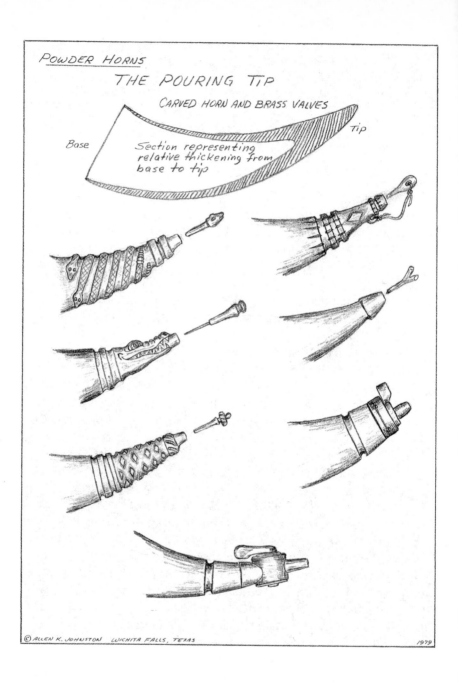

POWDER HORNS

THE POURING TIP

CARVED HORN AND BRASS VALVES

Base

Tip

Section representing relative thickening from base to tip

1979

PLATE 8

sea shells, leather, turtle shells, gourds, and from anything that was hollow or that could be made hollow.

Handling and storage of black gunpowder was a problem in the 1700s and 1800s. Powder was transported and stored in wooden kegs. Magazine quantities of the hygroscopic mixture could be kept in special buildings and shipboard compartments without being greatly affected by changes in humidity. Small quantities carried by traders and supplies kept by individuals often became soggy in moist, humid conditions and completely dried out over hot dry periods. Ideally, black gunpowder must have about 2 percent moisture content for best performance. Storekeepers and some traders used metal cans, specially designed and constructed, for storage of small stocks of powder. These cans were cylindrical from base to above mid-height, then cone shaped to a spout about four inches long and two inches in diameter. A handle was riveted to the side of the can and the spout was closed by a tight fitting metal cap. Many of these cans were made of copper and held about ten pounds of gunpowder.

Metal cans were superior to wooden kegs because they did not allow entry or exit of moisture, but condensation within the can was undesirable. Horn, however, allowed neither the penetration of moisture nor the build-up of condensation. It is for this reason that horn was the sought-after material for use as a powder flask. Great horns were imported from Africa and were prized by river traders for their stores of powder. Caches could be established at various locations along the trade route where gunpowder could be buried for months in oilskin wrapped horns. Under similar conditions powder in kegs would be worthless within a short time.

Flasks were used to carry other things besides gunpowder. They were used to carry such necessities of life and survival as water, salt, shot, herbs and medicines, oil, grease, and trap scents. By 1700, stoppered glass and ceramic bottles, jars and jugs, as well as tinned sheet metal and copper cans and boxes from England were finding their way to the frontier. The containers were scarce but those that reached the mountain man were put to good use as long as they were serviceable.

Indians were masters at innovation when they were faced with need of a container for food or water. Almost anything could be

33

POWDER HORNS
WOOD TIPS, BASE PLUGS, AND STOPPERS

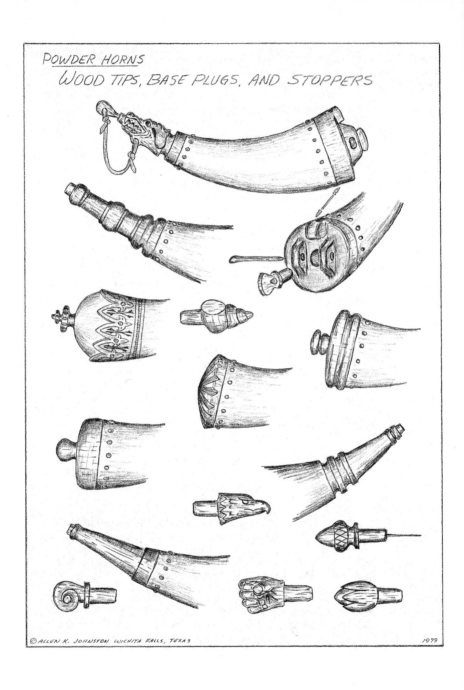

© ALLEN K. JOHNSTON WICHITA FALLS, TEXAS

1979

PLATE 9

done with materials occurring naturally in their habitat. The mountain man exchanged his knowledge of eighteenth and nineteenth century technology with these people of the Stone Age with resulting benefit to both. The two cultures blended well as long as there was peace. Cultural exchange accounts for the overlap of design in clothing and accouterments with the mountain man and plainsman appearing more Indian than colonial.

Some of the imaginative innovations our forefathers incorporated into their equipment were strokes of genius. Think of how many times you have stuck your hand with that vent pick in your possible bag. I have, many times. I solved the problem for a time by pressing the pick into the pith core of an ash shoot. The shoot dried and the pick slid out again and drew blood. I just took the stabbings as part of the game. Well, about 300 years ago, somebody realized the problem and installed his vent pick into the end of his powder horn stopper, out of harm's way, and never stuck himself again. I tried this innovation and now use and like it so well that I am passing it on to you. Nobody holds a patent on the powder horn, it has been around too long.

How do we go about making that one-of-a-kind flask or powder horn? Start with a pencil and a piece of paper and draw pictures. Try several different designs and shapes. Look at the horns that the shooters are carrying at the next blackpowder and smokepole club shoot. Sketch what you like or what catches your eye and incorporate that into your set of drawings. Go to the library, museum, or gun show and look and sketch some more. One day the sketches will gel and your idea will be firmly set in your mind. The first phase of making that horn will be off and running. Next, locate a suitable cow or buffalo horn and go to work.

Cow horn is the same material, biologically as well as chemically, as our fingernails. The physical characteristics are the same also. Horn will tend to be brittle when cold and dry, flexible when warm and moist, and soft and tender when soaked in hot water. Keep these properties in mind when working horn and they will keep you out of trouble and make the job easier.

The shape of a horn can be changed from an irregular oval, found in nature, to round by placing the horn in boiling water until it is soft and pliable enough to cover over a wood form. Work fast

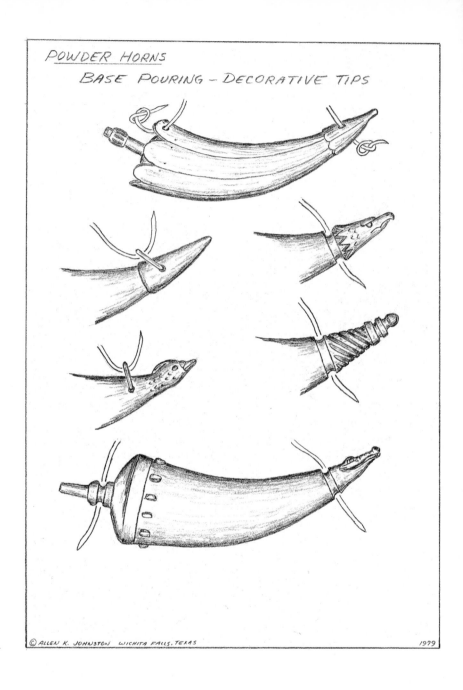

POWDER HORNS

BASE POURING - DECORATIVE TIPS

1979

PLATE 10

because, as the horn rapidly cools and dries, it will lose its pliability and become harder to work. The skirt of a cow horn is soft enough to trim with heavy duty scissors immediately after it is taken out of boiling water. This makes trimming the horn square across the base much easier than the hacksaw and file method. Forming a horn into a flat flask requires more boiling time but makes an interesting flask.

Scrape the horn when it is warm and moist. The cutting tool will cut cleanly during scraping rather than to gouge and tear the thin layers of horn. Sanding and polishing horn is best accomplished when the horn is dry and cold. The grit cuts faster and the finished surface takes on a brighter shine.

Sawing horn should be done with the horn warm and moist. There is less danger of cracking, tearing, or splitting the material under the stress of sawing. The teeth of the saw will clog if the horn is too tender, but this condition will not last long — as horn cools and toughens rapidly. Try to saw slowly to keep the blade and work from overheating. A hot blade will clog and seize the work, generally causing something to break at the wrong place, creating unwanted problems. Drilling should be done with a hand drill to reduce overheating of bit and horn.

Ornamental carving of horn may be done two ways, relief carving and scrimshaw carving. Relief carving is done with various cutting blades and files to produce deeply incised patterns, much like wood carving. Scrimshaw carving is done by making scratches or shallow cuts in the polished surface of the horn with a needle awl, then filling the work with a dark medium such as India ink. The ink brings out the pattern or picture and is permanent. Shading and highlighting is achieved by spacing the cuts or scratches. More color density is concentrated in areas of closely spaced scratches, much like the shading of printed photographs in newspapers where contrast is achieved by the spacing of dots. Scrimshaw work is a real art but with some practice it can be done reasonably well by the novice. Try it on a powder horn sometime. The results are rewarding. Lay out a pattern and work it in with a sharp pointed needle awl. Apply India ink by working it into the cuts with the end of the finger then polish away the excess with a soft cloth. When the horn has been covered with scrimshaw, scrape

POWDER HORNS

CARVED HORN POWDER VALVE

A DOWNY WOODPECKER

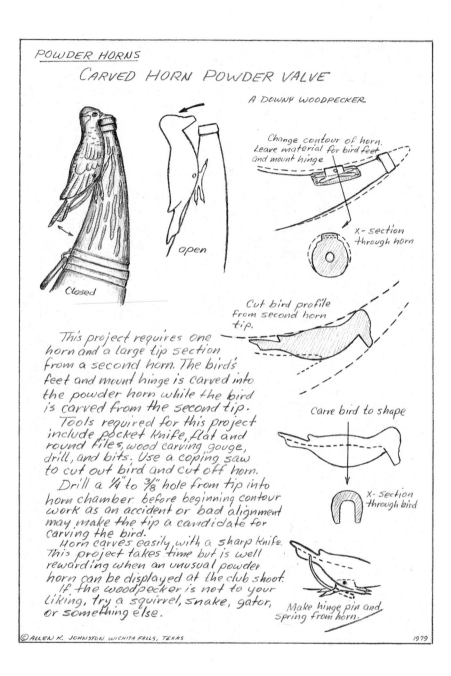

Change contour of horn. Leave material for bird feet and mount hinge

x-section through horn

Closed

open

Cut bird profile from second horn tip.

Carve bird to shape

x-section through bird

This project requires one horn and a large tip section from a second horn. The bird's feet and mount hinge is carved into the powder horn while the bird is carved from the second tip.

Tools required for this project include pocket knife, flat and round files, wood carving gouge, drill, and bits. Use a coping saw to cut out bird and cut off horn.

Drill a 1/4" to 3/8" hole from tip into horn chamber before beginning contour work as an accident or bad alignment may make the tip a candidate for carving the bird.

Horn carves easily with a sharp knife. This project takes time but is well rewarding when an unusual powder horn can be displayed at the club shoot.

If the woodpecker is not to your liking, try a squirrel, snake, gator, or something else.

Make hinge pin and spring from horn.

© ALLEN K. JOHNSTON WICHITA FALLS, TEXAS

1979

PLATE II

38

the horn down and polish it once more. Lay out a few patterns and try again. The same horn can be used through many practice sessions, then prepared once more for a finished job.

Now that you are ready to get started on that first powder horn, remember, take your time and enjoy the project, don't get in a hurry. Pay close attention to details like drilling holes through the horn using a bit slightly larger than the nail that passes through it. This keeps the horn from splitting or cracking during the final stages of assembly. Equally important is drilling the wood plug or base to which the horn is to be attached using a bit slightly smaller than the nails or brads to be used. These holes must be deep enough to accept the full length of the nails so that the plug is not split. I'm mentioning this because I know that the closer a project comes to completion, the more likely it is that disaster will overtake the job. It is human nature to get in a hurry and make a stupid blunder near the end of a project. Patience is the key to a successful job.

POWDER FLASKS

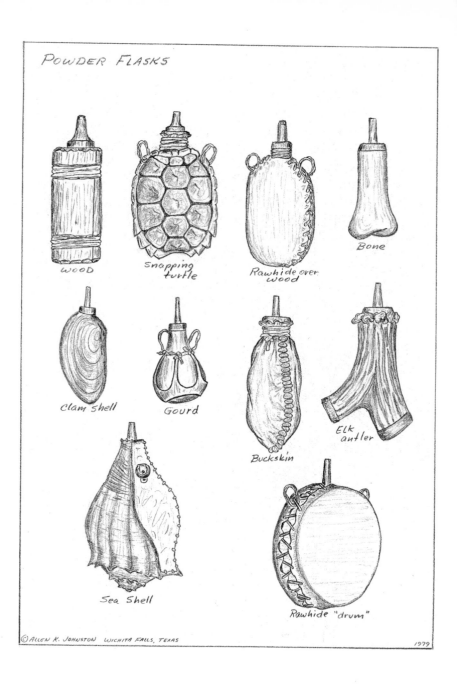

wood

Snapping turtle

Rawhide over wood

Bone

Clam shell

Gourd

Buckskin

Elk antler

Sea Shell

Rawhide "drum"

1979

PLATE 12

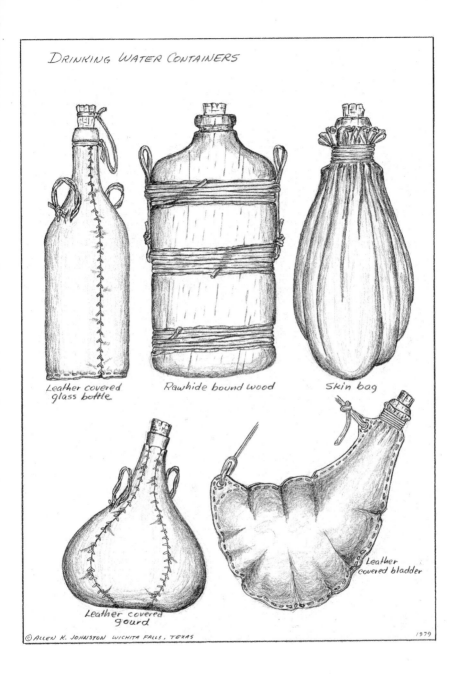

DRINKING WATER CONTAINERS

Leather covered
glass bottle

Rawhide bound wood

Skin bag

Leather covered
gourd

Leather
covered bladder

© ALLEN K. JOHNSTON WICHITA FALLS, TEXAS

1979

PLATE 13

HORNCRAFT PROJECTS

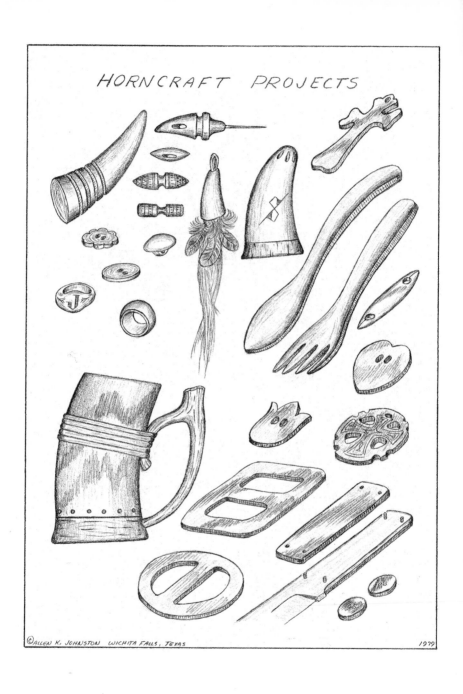

1979

PLATE 14

Knives

Weapons and tools used in the development and expansion of civilization are always of interest to the historian. Knives seem to hold the greatest fascination of any weapon or tool of history. Many books have been written in which knives have been classified and dated according to shapes, designs, and materials. The books may not agree, and you may not agree with the books, but one fact cannot be disputed; knives have been personal tools and weapons since the dawn of civilization. Materials have changed with the evolution of technology, but the basic instrument remains unchanged. It is a blade with a handle. There have been no revolutionary improvements in blade shape and design since the Stone Age.

Single edge blade? Double edge blade? Drop point? Clip point? Concavo-convex edges on the same blade? Big blade? Tiny blade? All of these designs and many more exist in collections of Stone Age artifacts. Then, how could Colonel James Bowie invent the obscenely large implement that bears his name today if he lived in the nineteenth century? The Roman soldier that reshaped his broken short sword to what we would call a clip point was too late to claim credit for the design. That soldier did, however, fill his need for a useable weapon until the legion could return to a source of supply. Perhaps he was so impressed by the shorter, more easily handled implement that he continued to carry it as a personal weapon, even after he was issued a new sword.

Westward expansion in America created an increasing demand for tools and implements. Among the implements sorely needed were knives and axes. The cutlers of Sheffield employed every available stove to produce blades. Most of the blades were consigned to shipment without handles and, being of poorer general

43

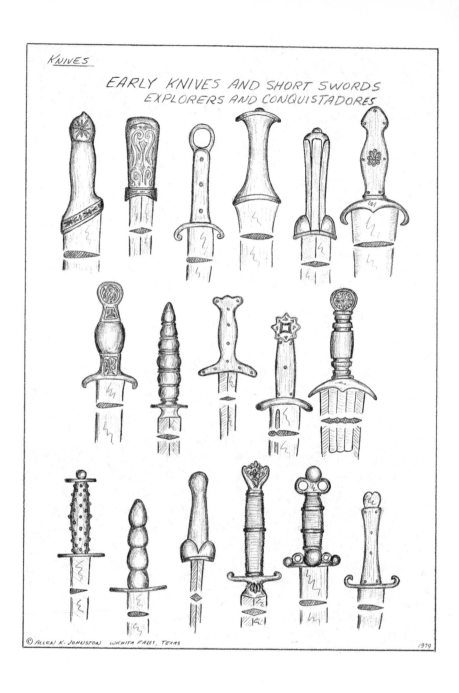

KNIVES

EARLY KNIVES AND SHORT SWORDS
EXPLORERS AND CONQUISTADORES

© ALLEN K. JOHNSTON   WICHITA FALLS, TEXAS   1979

PLATE 15

44

quality, were much less expensive than finished knives. The cutlers, however, reaped greater profits by being able to meet demands without hiring additional finish craftsmen. In addition to the profits made on the blades, the cutlers conducted business as usual by filling the normal needs of their trade with finished cutlery. Some finished knives reached the colonies but were so expensive that few could afford them. Perhaps this explains the apparent scarcity of artistically completed English-made knives of the 1600s and 1700s.

American completion of imported blades featured common style handles, mostly wood or antler. A few knives were finished by tinkers and silversmiths using artistic skills and fine materials. Some of these knives confound identification and classification because the craftsmen often used style characteristics of their homelands. Several knives classified as German, French, and Scottish imports were made in the colonies.

A local source of cutlery on the frontier was the blacksmith's forge. Suitable steel for knife making was scarce and so expensive that broken saber blades, cutting tools, etc., were premium finds and jealously hoarded. Occasionally, a smith made a knife on special order, but the general lack of materials restricted this source of blades. The picture changed by the early 1800s when steel became available from American mills. Continuing demand for blades stimulated greater local activity among smiths resulting in the establishment of an American cutlery industry. By 1850, Sheffield was flooding the country with completed Bowie knives. Westward expansion was rapidly increasing, the gold rush was on, and unrest over slavery all created a growing market.

Today, the United States is not engaged in any war, the slavery issue was settled a century ago, the gold fields are worked out, and the country is fully expanded to both natural and political borders, but still the demand for sheath knives runs high. There are more cutlers in the United States today than at any time in American History. The answer to the enigma lies in the romance of days long passed. The knife, in its many shapes and designs, is a symbol that stimulates the imagination. Whether they will admit it or not, millions of people in this country are caught up in the romanticism of history.

KNIVES OF THE AMERICAN FRONTIER
1700 — 1850

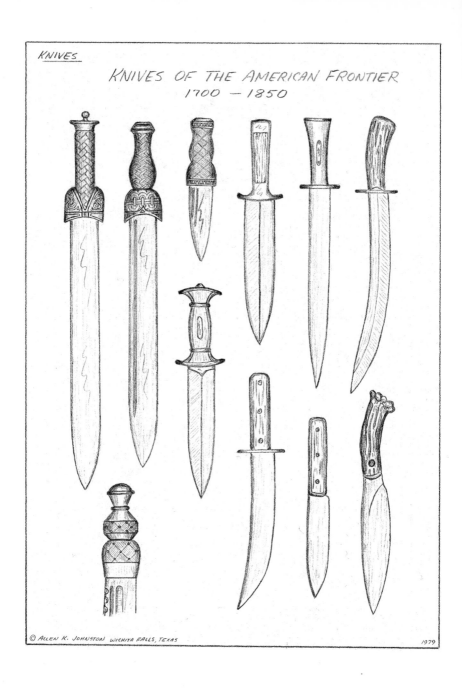

1979

PLATE 16

Selecting a knife to go with a costume for a particular period of American history may pose a problem. It would be considered heresy to outfit in a costume of the 1650s and add, for the finishing touch, a carbine bayonet and sheath from World War II. Almost any custom knife maker will take an order for a special design, for a price, and make delivery one to nine months later. The easiest, as well as the most interesting and enjoyable, way out of the dilemma is to rework the bayonet and make a suitable sheath. The work starts in the public library.

Research the implements of the 1600s and make sketches of the designs and characteristics common to knives and sheaths of the period. Handle designs carry over from century to century with only minor changes. Some handles identified as fourteenth century have carried over into the twentieth century. Catalog the materials used in handles and sheaths of the period of interest. Horn, bone, shell, antler, wood, cord, and leather were commonly used materials of the 1600s. Ivory, jade, precious metals and stones, exotic leathers and fabrics, etc., were affordable only by nobility and would be out of character for a New England settler or a French trapper.

Once a pattern has been selected, remove the handle from the bayonet and study the tang to see what has to be done to make the new handle fit. There is enough steel in the carbine bayonet blade to make a dagger that is reasonably authentic. The steel will be superior to the steel of the 1600s but it will have to do. Carefully grind or file the back of the blade to an edge matching the bevel and taper of the existing edge. The new blade shape should be a flattened diamond or flat oval in cross section. Adapt the new handle to the reshaped blade and the result will be a dagger not too unlike one that Captain Miles Standish may have worn.

Whether you are costuming for a pageant or equipping for a stay in the wilderness, knives play an important role. If the ideal knife to fit the role can't be found, one has to be made or a make-do knife purchased. With the availability of preground and finished blades in a multitude of shapes and sizes, it may be foolish to make a blade from scratch. The preground blades are not expensive and, in many cases, can be altered in shape to fill your need. However, if you want to go all the way, I'll cheer you on. I've been the whole

47

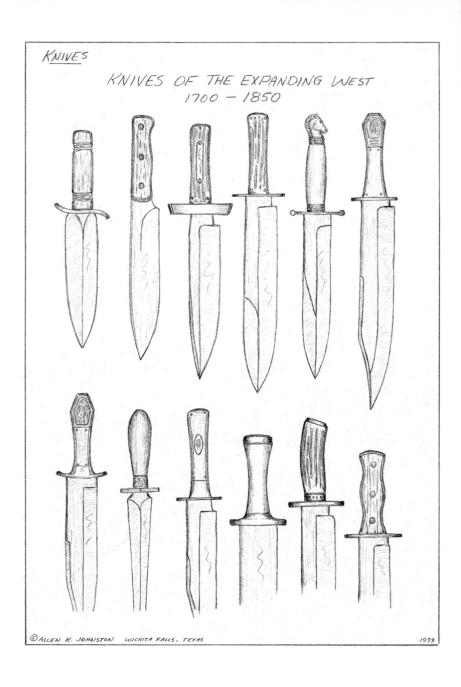

KNIVES

KNIVES OF THE EXPANDING WEST
1700 — 1850

©ALLEN K. JOHNSTON   WICHITA FALLS, TEXAS   1979

PLATE 17

Poured Rivets

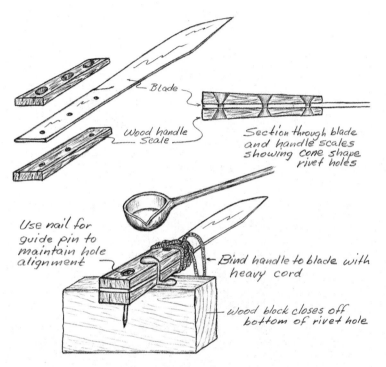

Blade

Wood handle
Scale

Section through blade
and handle scales
showing cone shape
rivet holes

Use nail for
guide pin to
maintain hole
alignment

Bind handle to blade with
heavy cord

Wood block closes off
bottom of rivet hole

Pour molten lead into center hole, remove nail and pour second hole, remove cord binding and pour last hole. File away excess lead then shape and finish handle.

Lead-tin solder, linotype metal, babbit, and zinc make stronger rivets than pure lead.

If handle works loose, rivets can be tightened by tapping with a hammer.

1979

PLATE 18

route: forging, grinding, tempering, drawing, polishing, and finishing. It is a lot of work, though quite rewarding and satisfying, to start with a bar of steel and wind up with a finished knife.

Many knives carried in the wilderness were put together without hilts. Hollow handles were the easiest to use because they required no drilling and pinning as do the scale handles. The hollow handle was filled with pitch, rosin, sulfur, or glue to set the blade. This was the best that they had, and they used it. If Daniel Boone had epoxy, he would have used epoxy. It is good sense to deviate from authenticity when it comes time to set the blade. The knife will be used for something, even if it is slicing watermelons at the blackpowder and smokepole club picnic, and you will want it to be safe. Tell the crowd that you set the handle with the world's finest pitch from the pines of Georgia, I'll help you swear to it, but set that handle to stay with epoxy and prevent an accident.

The wilderness pilgrim carried more than one knife. He carried a patch knife to service his rifle during loading and a hunting knife to clean and prepare his food, skin animals, and do the usual camp and cabin chores. Sometimes, when conditions warranted, he carried a long blade knife to serve as a short sword when an additional weapon was needed. A dagger in his legging or boot top was not uncommon when times were hard.

Each knife possessed different characteristics. The patch knife was small, usually with a straight or hooked blade. The straight blade was similar to a straight razor. In fact, many patch knives were old razors. The hooked blade was sharpened to cut on the inside of the hook. Some patch knives were sharpened only on one side of the blade so that the side riding the muzzle of the rifle remained flat. Blades were ground to a long wedge so that they sharpened easily and cut cleanly. Because knives were made out of anything available, they took on all shapes and, as long as they cut patches, nobody cared.

The classic hunting knife of the twentieth century is more representative of a dagger than the utility knife of the wilderness pilgrim. Hunting knives used well into the 1840s were light, thin bladed knives common to the cooking hearths of the frontier cabins. The thin blade was a natural selection because it took a keen edge and held it well, did not bind in deep cuts, handled easily, and was not expensive. Blades imported from England were patterns that served the people of Europe for generations. The working knife was the utility knife and the fighting knife was the heavy, thick-bladed dagger. Today, we find utility knives in the home kitchen and a poorly designed hunting dagger for utility use in the field. There are several utility patterns available that have been ground to authentic early American designs. These blades make fine costume pieces and excellent hunting knives for field or camp.

The long knife was a weapon, made for killing. The blade was about a foot in length and was stiff and sturdy. It was sharpened along one edge and was ground to a long, sharp point. The long Scots dirk had been in use in Scotland some 300 years before the colonization of America and was ideal for the frontier and wilderness. Sheffield ground a blade for export that was based on the dirk. This pattern is available today as the flintlock rifleman's knife, an authentic reproduction of the originals. Some of the long knives were made out of broken or cut-off saber blades. The dirk and long knife were used to deliver thrusts and slashes in much the same manner as the saber was used.

The late-comer to the knives of the frontier came from Louisiana by way of Texas, or so the story goes. There are so many theories of how the Bowie knife came to be, and where it came from, that I'll not even enter into the discussion. Anyway, that ruckus we had at the Alamo and carried over to San Jacinto sure made the Bowie knife popular. It was a short sword, a broad ax, and a club all forged in one piece. The Bowie replaced both the long knife and tomahawk and has enjoyed a popularity lasting a century-and-a-half. Colonel James Bowie was killed in the battle of the Alamo in 1836, and before his bones were cold Bowie knives from the cutlers of Sheffield were flooding the country.

Knives and tomahawks supplemented the long rifle in combat. The soldier, frontiersman, and pioneer derived a great confidence knowing that he was armed as well as times would permit and that his chances of survival were increased, even if only slightly. In reality, their chances for survival were greatly increased through their increased self-confidence. Psychologists contend that the obscenely large knives carried by fighting men are no more than phallus symbols, mere tokens or charms of superstition. Some short swords and daggers of ancient times actually mounted a carved phallus for a handle. Sex symbols were signs of virility and manliness that, to the superstitious, were supposed to ward off evil and protect a man in battle. Personally, I think that superstitions are ridiculous and totally unsupported, but under life and death conditions I want a phallus symbol-mounted eight inch blade because I'm going to need all the help I can get!

The sketches making up the knife plates are mostly handle forms. Blade shapes and comparative lengths are shown on a few sketches to illustrate size and length of a few classics to that period. Early daggers averaged about six inches in blade length and had many blade styles but these weapons were chiefly piercing instruments and were not restricted to flat-ground blades. Cross sections of the blades are shown in sketch form, with an inset on the blade below the hilt.

The Knife Sheath

The belt knife is as much a part of the historic costume as a pair of pants. In fact, a lot of buckskinners I know would rather parade around without their pants than without that great Bowie knife. Much thought and planning goes into selecting a knife to fill that void in the costume. Once the knife is selected, the problem is only half solved. What are you going to carry it in? What kind of sheath goes with the period you plan to portray? Is the planned sheath safe?

We practice safety on the firing line, but remember, that three pound Bowie will cleave half your foot off if it falls from your belt and lands just right on your moccasin. Plan some sort of a cover, catch, or tie into the construction of the sheath. It is not necessary to have a short sword ready at all times because most club ranges are reasonably safe from grizzly bears. The knife should be secured in the sheath and some feature to reduce the chance of the blade penetrating the side of the sheath should be included. A long, narrow, sharp pointed blade is more likely to pierce the side of a leather sheath than a broad blade. I have seen more than one knife go through the side of a sheath. In one incident, two-thirds of a blade was exposed as the result of a fall. Fortunately, there was no injury, but there have been similar incidents that resulted in blood loss.

Knife sheath materials of wood, rawhide, and leather will fit all Early American costumes from 1620 through 1850. Combinations of these materials were used in all periods, mainly because they were readily accessible and in abundant supply. The strength of materials and their resistance to piercing and cutting ranges from wood, as the most resistant, to leather as the least. Most of

MAKING A WOOD AND RAWHIDE KNIFE SHEATH

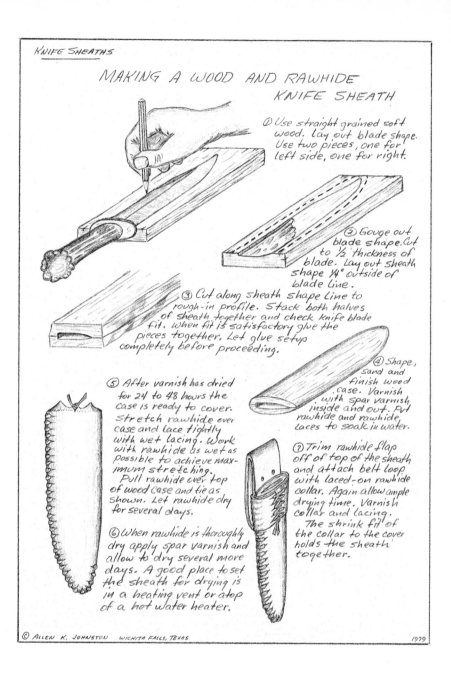

① Use straight grained soft wood. Lay out blade shape. Use two pieces, one for left side, one for right.

② Gouge out blade shape. Cut to ½ thickness of blade. Lay out sheath shape ¼" outside of blade line.

③ Cut along sheath shape line to rough-in profile. Stack both halves of sheath together and check knife blade fit. When fit is satisfactory glue the pieces together. Let glue setup completely before proceeding.

④ Shape, sand and finish wood case. Varnish with spar varnish, inside and out. Put rawhide and rawhide laces to soak in water.

⑤ After varnish has dried for 24 to 48 hours the case is ready to cover. Stretch rawhide over case and lace tightly with wet lacing. Work with rawhide as wet as possible to achieve maximum stretching. Pull rawhide over top of wood case and tie as shown. Let rawhide dry for several days.

⑥ When rawhide is thoroughly dry apply spar varnish and allow to dry several more days. A good place to set the sheath for drying is in a heating vent or atop of a hot water heater.

⑦ Trim rawhide flap off of top of the sheath and attach belt loop with laced-on rawhide collar. Again allow ample drying time. Varnish collar and lacing. The shrink fit of the collar to the cover holds the sheath together.

© ALLEN K. JOHNSTON   WICHITA FALLS, TEXAS

1979

PLATE 19

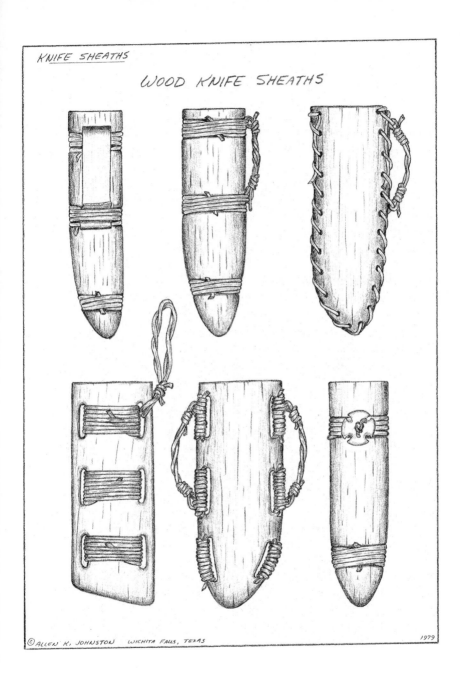

KNIFE SHEATHS

WOOD KNIFE SHEATHS

©ALLEN K. JOHNSTON   WICHITA FALLS, TEXAS   1979

PLATE 20

55

WOOD AND RAWHIDE SHEATHS

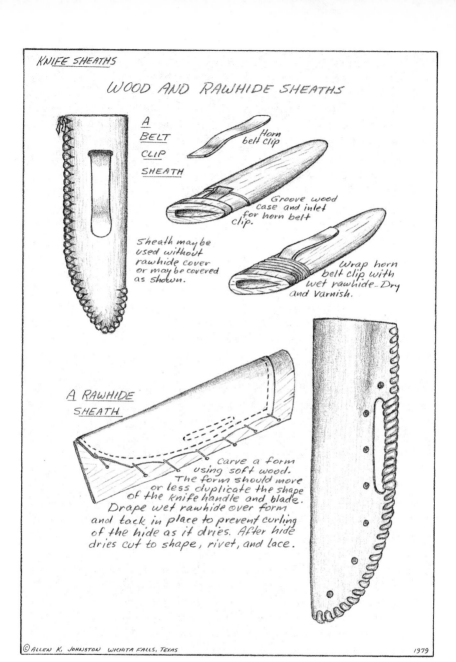

A BELT CLIP SHEATH

Horn belt clip

Groove wood case and inlet for horn belt clip.

Sheath may be used without rawhide cover or may be covered as shown.

Wrap horn belt clip with wet rawhide. Dry and Varnish.

A RAWHIDE SHEATH

Carve a form using soft wood. The form should more or less duplicate the shape of the knife handle and blade. Drape wet rawhide over form and tack in place to prevent curling of the hide as it dries. After hide dries cut to shape, rivet, and lace.

© ALLEN K. JOHNSTON WICHITA FALLS, TEXAS

1979

PLATE 21

56

the time, I use a combination of two materials to make a sheath, but sometimes I use all three in the same sheath.

The wood case provides a hard and stiff liner for either of the other two materials. A beaded soft buckskin cover over the wood case makes a very attractive sheath and eliminates some of the hazards common to buckskin sheaths alone. Sometimes, trying to find a way to make the liner stay in place inside of a leather cover, or finding a method of attachment to the belt tests your ingenuity. Don't worry, whatever you invent to do the job was probably an old and accepted method by 1700. Remember, we are only rediscovering these methods.

Rawhide liners can be sandwiched between layers of heavy leather to strengthen the sheath. Stitch or rivet the rawhide in place when it is wet. This will wet the leather adjacent to the liner. Slide in a carved wood form, similar to the shape of the blade, and let the sheath dry. After removal of the wood form, the dry rawhide will retain the form of the blade and take on the strength and stiffness of thin wood. Using this method, you will have a perfect fitting, reasonably safe sheath.

When using leather by itself, use the heaviest grade available and, if practical, use double thickness. If it is impractical to use double thickness over the entire sheath, it may be possible to incorporate a double layer over the toe of the sheath where the knife point usually tears through. In fact, it wouldn't be cheating to use a metal toe, either outside or under the leather—it was done this way well before 1620.

Let's be consistent. If we are going to demand safety on the firing line, then let's have it behind the firing line as well. Maybe this all sounds like an overprotective scoutmaster cautioning his troop before an outing. Safety is no laughing matter, it is just good sense. Besides, many of us learned knife and ax safety in the boy scout program and still practice and preach it.

LEATHER AND RAWHIDE SHEATHS

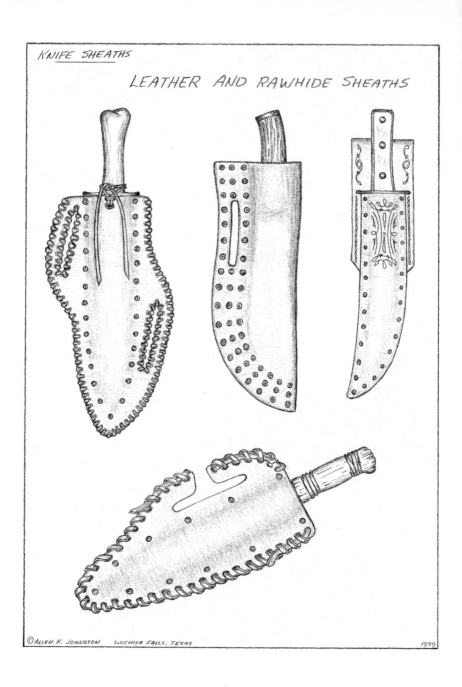

©ALLEN K. JOHNSTON   WICHITA FALLS, TEXAS   1979

PLATE 22

58

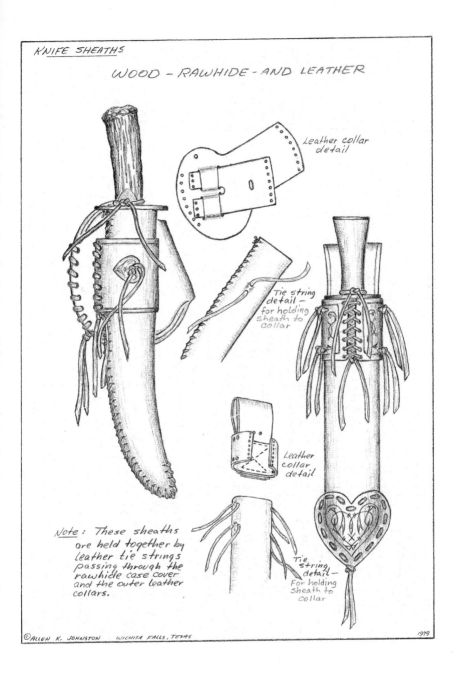

KNIFE SHEATHS

WOOD - RAWHIDE - AND LEATHER

Leather collar detail

Tie string detail – for holding sheath to collar

Leather collar detail

Note: These sheaths are held together by leather tie strings passing through the rawhide case cover and the outer leather collars.

Tie string detail – For holding sheath to collar

©ALLEN K. JOHNSTON   WICHITA FALLS, TEXAS   1979

PLATE 23

Tomahawk Sockets and Covers

Captain Robert Rogers issued standing orders to his company of rangers in which the tomahawk was specifically mentioned. Tomahawks were to be kept scoured and sharp. This was not just military busy-work but serious business. The French were at war with the British and had allied themselves with the Indians so that the Continental army, along with a few British regulars, had a real fight on their hands. Rogers knew that a bright and shining blade would draw the attention of an enemy more than a tarnished blade, and that if the attention could be momentarily distracted there would be an opportunity of striking a fatal blow. When the stroke was made, the blade had to be sharp enough to finish the job in one lick.

The green buckskin clad ranger carried his tomahawk at his belt, usually hanging from a loop or socket. Sometimes it was carried in a loop affixed to the possible bag, or hanging from a separate strap over the shoulder. Some even carried the 'hawk stuck through the belt. However it was carried, it was carried securely because death could be the price paid for losing it.

A sharp edge hanging at the side of a man on the march created an opportunity for a cut hand, arm, or leg and so was protected until it became apparent that the tomahawk may be needed at any moment. For the rangers, the blade was probably uncovered as they left the sanctuary of their river island base, as a hostile scouting party or strike force could be in the area at any time.

Tomahawks had other uses besides being a weapon. They were used as hand axes or hatchets for any and all chores on the trail. The blade was kept sharp enough to skin out an elk without the need of a knife. Boughs and saplings fell easily under the blade when time came to erect a temporary shelter or make a frame to

TOMAHAWK SOCKETS

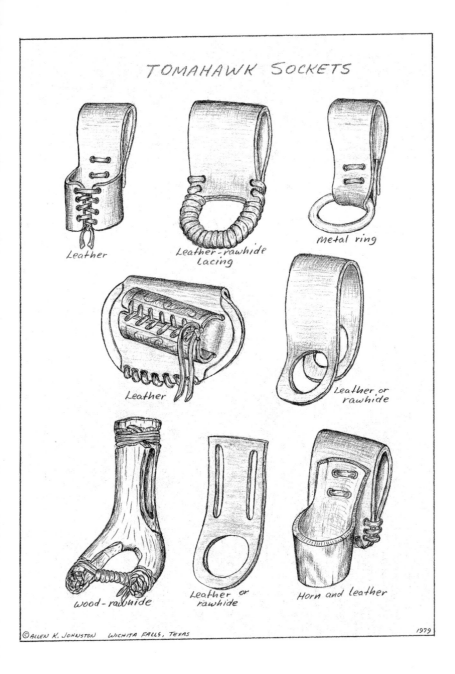

Leather

Leather-rawhide
lacing

Metal ring

Leather

Leather or
rawhide

Wood-rawhide

Leather or
rawhide

Horn and leather

1979

PLATE 24

stretch a hide. The 'hawk was considered so valuable in the wilderness that it was never abused. Heavy cutting always went to the ax.

The sport of throwing the tomahawk has always been popular. It was done at rendezvous to show off individual ability at arms contest, the same as shooting the mark with the rifle or pistol. To throw the tomahawk, or knife, in combat was to disarm one's self at a time when weapons were needed most.

TOMAHAWK COVERS

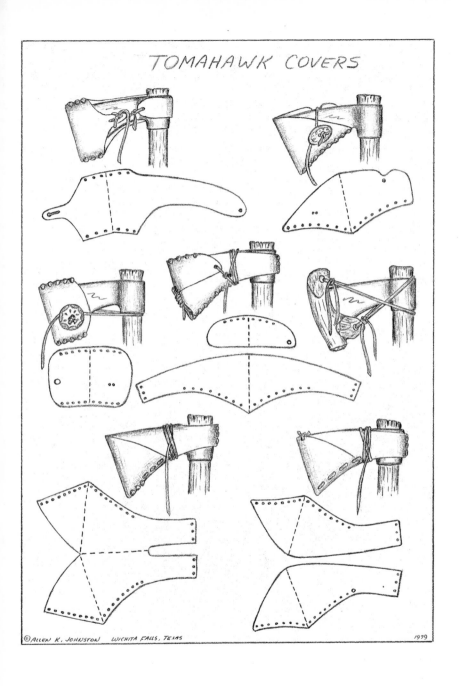

1979

PLATE 25

Rawhide

Rawhide is a material that is generally overlooked for accessory items to period costumes and equipment. Rawhide was the sheet metal and bailing wire of the wilderness and frontier. Because no tanning was involved, rawhide was readily available whether taken from a fresh kill or stripped from a carcass bloating in the sun. In fact, the pioneers found that an old carcass was better if they could stand the smell. The hair on the ripe hide would slip off easily and, after the hide dried, it didn't smell too bad.

The frontiersman prepared his rawhide in the simplest manner possible. A fresh skin was carefully cleaned of all meat and fat, then laid on the ground hair side up. Cold ashes from the fire pit were spread over the hide and worked into the hair with water to form a thick paste. The hide was then folded and stored in a cool, moist place where it was kept wet for three or four days. After the wood ash had time to work, the hide was unfolded and placed hairside up on a smooth beam made from a peeled log. A piece of tree limb with the bark removed was forcefully drawn with the lay of the hair to slip the hair from the skin. Following removal of the hair, the skin was carefully washed in clear water then stretched to a frame to dry. The dried skin was said to be in the "flint stage" and would not ruin as long as it was kept dry. Sometimes rawhide was prepared with the hair left in place. After cleaning off the meat and fat, the skin was stretched on a frame to dry without any further preparation. Modern day frontiersmen may wish to utilize lime obtained from the local lumber yard to form the thick paste. Warning—please wear gloves and mask.

Rawhide is not a pretty material, but neither is a mill cut, kiln dried slab of walnut. Any natural material must be turned into something useful or skillfully and artistically combined with other

Above: A group of Red River Renegades.

Right: Laine "Two Crow" Crowe lookin' good.

Right: Ken and Robbie Matlock pose in full gear. Many enjoyable hours go into putting together that "just right" outfit.

Below: Some people are just not sociable till they get their morning cup of coffee. Isn't that right Wade Nickens?

Bottom: Bolo tie with face of sun god carved in the base of a deer antler. Antler tip secured with rawhide is used as a button for this buckskin outfit. Crafted by the author.

Top left: Mike "Iron Mike" Middleworth using a pipe to kindle the flames (saves the beard).

Top right: The works. Crafted by the author.

Right: Glenn "Tree" Wood. Outfits are as unique as the people wearing them.

Pocket tinder box with leather belt pouch. Crafted by the author.

A unique quiver.

Robbie Matlock in her buckskins.

Janie Gonzales working dough for tortillas.

Typical cooking set up. Notice the bake kettle hanging from the spit. This is but one of many ways to use this versatile vessel.

Laine "Two Crow" Crowe and Mike "Iron Mike" Middleworth making fry bread.

Top: Packing in for the hunt.

Left: Grey Coat—Bob "Reb" Neal.

Below: Terry's 8th Texas—standing: Fred McNeil, Jimmy Chadwell, Billy Hibbs, Lewis Iselin, John Roberts, Jim Lackey, Bob Neal, William Iselin (flag boy). Kneeling: Mike Pence, Wade Nickens, Roger Fowler.

A few Red River Renegades visit Austin, Texas.

Left: Robbie, Ken and Mickey Matlock. Right: Ken Matlock in capote and fur cap with bear claw necklace.

Bottom: Possibilities for the possible bag—basic contents with powder horn.

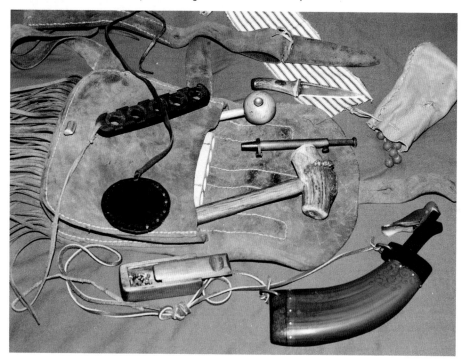

Roger Fowler finds he has too much gun for so little a target.

Left: Youngsters also enjoy the pageantry. Bobby "Critter" Scobee with his turtle pouch.

Bottom: Tino "Broken Arrow" Gonzales.

Above: Mike "Animal" Pence poses in full gear.

Right: Amanda Matlock all decked out.

Bottom: Many styles and qualities of bags can be purchased or made.

Above: Some accouterments of interest: notice the bear jaw knife, intricate beadwork, and bear claw necklace.

Below: Roger Fowler's all set for Thanksgiving.

Left: Glenn "Tree" Wood preparing to "shoot from the bag."

Below: Mike "Animal" Pence with daughter Tori.

Paul and Cindy Gwynn.

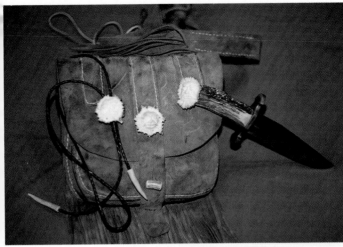

Sun god carved in deer antler. Crafted by the author.

Darrel Johnston hard at work.

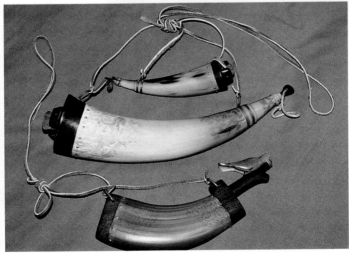

Notice the scrimshaw work on these powder horns crafted by the author.

Left: Billy Hibbs in his buckskins.

Below: Vendor's blanket displays decorated cow skulls, beaded pouches, and bearskins.

Below: A few of the knives crafted by the author.

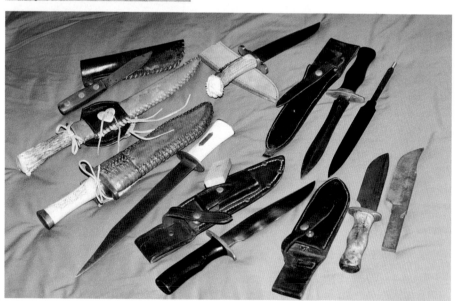

Top: This group is enjoying coffee and early morning meditation at Henry's Fork, Green River in Wyoming.

Left: Shelters of all types are seen at the rendezvous.

Below: A group of Renegades help promote Underwoods BBQ.

Above: A contrast of buckskin and cloth clothing. Laine "Two Crow" Crowe and Charlie "One Eye" Coker prepare for the hunt.

Right: Rhonda Scobee prepares the potatoes.

Below: Bob "Reb" Neal with grandson Bobby "Critter" Scobee. Reb's caplock single shot pistol is attached to his belt.

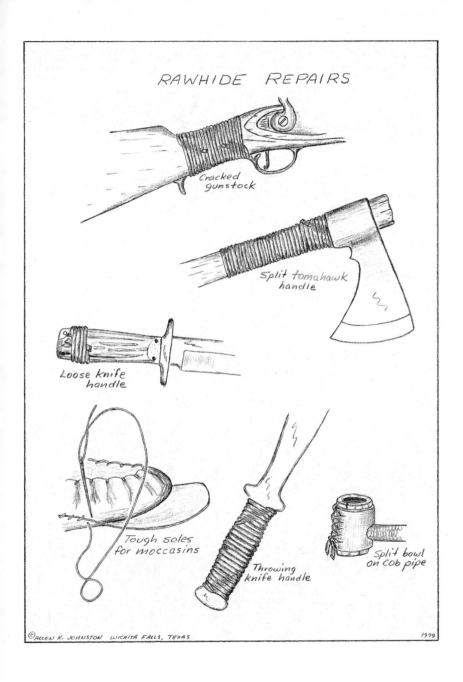

RAWHIDE REPAIRS

Cracked gunstock

Split tomahawk handle

Loose knife handle

Tough soles for moccasins

Throwing knife handle

Split bowl on cob pipe

1979

PLATE 26

A RAINPROOF LARDER

Rawhide covered wood box.
Leather strap hasp and hinges.
Rope lifting handles.

Nailing and tacking of box and cover are more modern than rawhide lacing. Older boxes were put together with thin light wood using laced rawhide joints. Cover and hinges were laced to the box. No metal fastenings were used. Making the laced box takes a little more time and is more fragile. Remember – someone is going to sit on the box sometime.

Miter Joint

Drill and lace

←Lid
←Box

Lid forms a weather cover by overlap fit.

Cover assembled box with wet rawhide. Stretch hide as tightly as possible.

Sandpaper all boards, round all edges and remove all burrs from drill holes. Glued and nailed box should be sanded well after assembly. Varnish boards or assembled box before covering. Varnish will prevent warping.

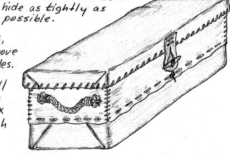

1979

PLATE 27

materials before it becomes pleasing to the eye. Buckskin is just buckskin until it is turned into a good-fitting shirt. Just because the material lacks aesthetic beauty, don't pass it by.

Rawhide has some interesting properties. When it is dry, it is hard, tough, and flexible. Soak rawhide in water for several hours and it becomes soft and supple, and can be stretched about 30 percent larger than its dry dimensions. After wet hide is stretched over a form it tries to resume its original dimension as it dries, and draws tightly to the form. Dry rawhide is translucent and can be used to replace a window pane. It will let light in and fill the open hole to keep the wind out. It makes a beautiful lamp shade for that just right decorator lamp in the den. Greased rawhide is pliable and turns water well. Oilskins were the forerunners of the raincoat and plastic sheeting.

Rawhide has been used in saddle making for centuries, to make almost indestructible saddle trees and pack saddles. Sailors used hide in the rigging of ships to protect the halyards and stays from wear and chafing. Magellan and his crew had to eat the rawhide rigging of their ship to keep from starving to death as they circumnavigated the world in the early 1500s. Gold miners of California, Colorado, and New Mexico lashed their flumes and sluices together with hide lashings. Historically, as a material beneficial to the needs of man, rawhide predates the discovery of fire.

The uses of rawhide in pioneering and repairs are limitless. Many items of personal use can be fashioned from the material. Several rawhide projects and uses are illustrated in plates throughout this book. Other suggestions for rawhide projects include: cutting small disks to be used for buttons, making small cones for feather and hair bangles, stiffeners for cap bills, backing to add strength and cast to a bow, braided to make rope, lashings for footbridges and towers, covering for shooting box and small containers, lashing for lodge poles, belts, belt hooks and buckles, shields and signs, drums, sandals, conchos, faces and masks, snowshoes, ski bindings, baskets and buckets, and harnesses.

Rediscover this neglected resource and consider using rawhide whenever possible for making and repairing items for the costume or camp. It is a material worth looking into.

Clothing

Clothing of the 1700s to the 1850s followed a varied pattern of fashion distribution. Social status in early America was reflected by dress. People of wealth or importance wore the latest fashions from England and France. The common people had to be frugal and wore clothes of durable fabrics, simple colors, and conservative cut. The majority of the people were common people and the clothing characteristic of the times was their mode of dress.

Homespun fabrics and buckskin made up the bulk of the garments worn in the frontier and wilderness America. Spinning wheels and looms were commonplace in homes and cabins. Community looms were housed in specially built cabins where as many as a dozen families would come to weave their yarns into fabric. Sometimes yarns would be left with a family owning a loom to have cloth woven on the halves. Cotton, wood, and flax fibers were carded and spun into yarns and woven into close mesh, durable fabric. The household dye pot was kept beside the fireplace. Imported dyes were available from indigo peddlers, but were expensive. Most of the homespun fabrics were dyed with the juices and extracts from forest and garden plants. Some of the plants used for dyes included: bayberry, yellow root, red oak, sassafras, and sweet-leaf for yellow dyes; walnut, gall-berry, and maple for brown and black; pokeberry for crimson; and iris blossoms for purple dye. Dark blue paper wrappers from loaf sugar were saved and boiled to make blue dye. Calico, which dates back to Europe well before the 1600s, was printed with hand carved wood block stamps.

Women of the frontier probably wore the least colorful attire of the era. Their skirts were long and full, hanging in folds from waist to hemline. Even though the skirt was cut full, no more fabric

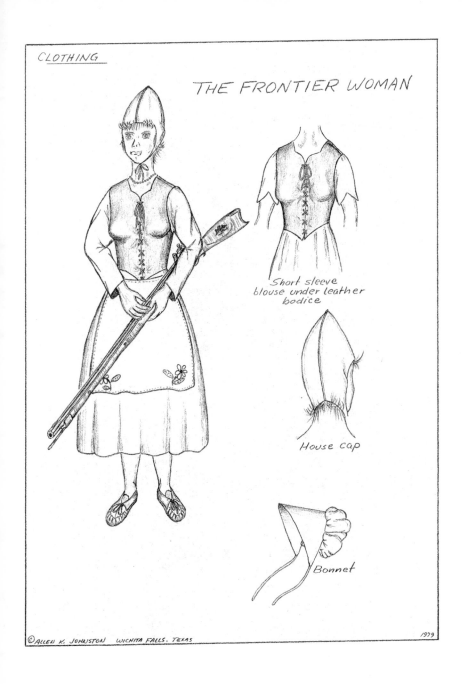

THE FRONTIER WOMAN

Short sleeve blouse under leather bodice

House cap

Bonnet

©ALLEN K. JOHNSTON   WICHITA FALLS. TEXAS   1979

PLATE 28

85

BUCKSKIN SQUAW DRESS

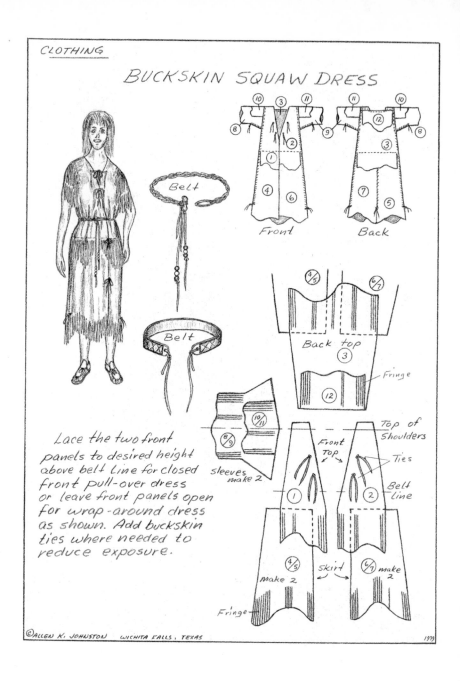

Belt

Belt

Front

Back

4/5   6/7

Back top
3

Fringe

12

Top of
Shoulders

Front
Top

Ties

Belt
Line

10/11

8/9

sleeves
make 2

1   2

4/5   6/7 make
2

Make 2   Skirt

Fringe

Lace the two front
panels to desired height
above belt line for closed
front pull-over dress
or leave front panels open
for wrap-around dress
as shown. Add buckskin
ties where needed to
reduce exposure.

©ALLEN K. JOHNSTON   WICHITA FALLS, TEXAS   1979

PLATE 29

86

was used than was absolutely necessary. In larger settlements and villages, the skirt was worn with the hemline at the ankles. Shorter skirts, with the hemline striking near mid-calf, were common to the more strenuous life of small settlements and wilderness living. The color of the skirt was usually dark blue or black.

Blouses were loosely cut with short sleeves for indoor wear and long sleeves for outdoors and cooler weather. They were finished without collars or frills, to conserve cloth, and were bleached white or dyed very light colors. A bodice made of heavy fabric, leather, or buckskin was often worn. The bodice covered the blouse and laced down the front. The garment was often dyed a dark color, although natural colors were not unusual.

For housework and chores, a knee-length, white linen apron was worn tied about the waist. The pioneer woman had several aprons, some were plain and others were embroidered with colorful borders and flowered designs. Kerchiefs and house caps were worn indoors, as much to keep the head warm as to protect the woman's hair. Fancy hair styles had no place in the frontier. The woman wore her hair moderately long, plaited into braids, and coiled up on top of her head. As the chill of the evening descended on the cabin or the weather cooled, a shawl of appropriate weight was worn over her shoulders.

The women of the colonies and the frontier were always careful to protect their skin from the rays of the sun. They rarely went out into the sunshine without full protective covering. Long sleeves, bonnets, dusters, shawls, and other protective wraps were in general use throughout the country. Footwear varied according to climate and need. Shoes, moccasins, and even bare feet were common in and around the cabin when the weather permitted. As winter set in, boots and fur or blanket wraps were used to make life a little more bearable.

Feminine undergarments consisted of the camisole, or loosely fitting underwaist; the chemise, which was a shirt-like underblouse; and pantalets. Pantalets were below-the-knee length, loose drawers with a frill or ruffle at the bottom of each leg. The underclothing was fastened about the body with laces and drawstrings. Underskirts were seldom worn and were considered excessive.

Sometimes, a detachable frill, fastened to the inside of the skirt at the hem, was worn in place of the underskirt.

The arrival of winter brought with it the need for a warm outer garment. A classic cold weather wrap was the capuchin, or ankle-length hooded cloak. The hood was large and usually heavily padded and quilted. The cloak had a tightly woven wool outer shell with a thick wool blanket material lining. A fur collar was often incorporated into the capuchin. The cloak was sleeveless, sometimes with slits cut in the sides for extension of the arms, and closed down the front with wood or horn toggles.

Buckskin clothing for the frontier and wilderness woman, when worn, followed the same simple design of the dress of the Indian squaw. White women were seldom allowed to venture beyond the frontier settlements. Sensible husbands made their women-folk stay at home near the safety of the fort and neighbors.

Few of the frontier women owned jewelry except for, perhaps, a ring or locket which had been passed down through her family. Mourning rings were commonly given at funerals by the family of the deceased, if they were well-to-do, but these were put away after a period of mourning. It was in bad taste to wear such a ring as a personal adornment. Usually, the only ornamentation to the simple costume consisted of a small string of trade beads or a red ribbon.

Men's clothing included canvas or heavy corded trousers, usually without pockets. Knee britches, tied below the knee with laces or straps, and long pants were both common. The trousers were held up by a belt or suspenders. Men's pants were usually butternut, brown, blue, gray, or black.

Shirts were long sleeved, loose cut, and long tailed; and were appropriately called "long shirts." Some of the shirts were open, button front, while others were tunic front laced or buttoned at the neck. The long shirt was worn with the tail out and cinched about the waist with a belt, or with the tail tucked into the waistband or trousers. Cotton or linen fabric in solid colors and calico prints were used in making long shirts.

Footwear was dictated by occupation or activity. Boots or moccasins were commonly worn by the frontiersman. Leather leggings provided added protection to both legs and trousers.

The "hunting shirt" of the frontiersman was made of buckskin.

A PULL-OVER BUCKSKIN SHIRT

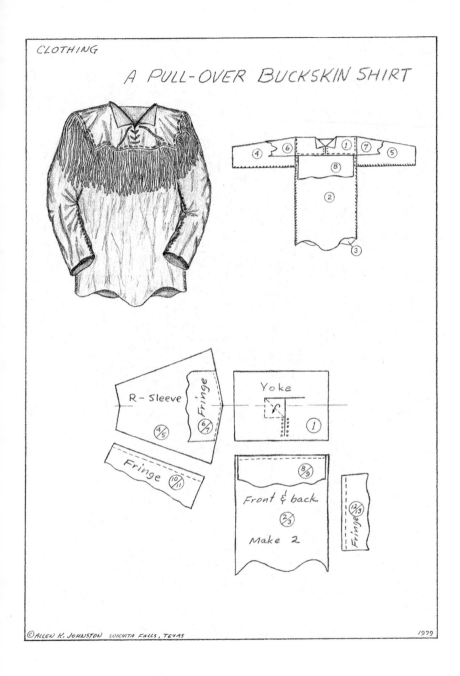

©ALLEN K. JOHNSTON WICHITA FALLS, TEXAS   1979

PLATE 30

89

OPEN FRONT BUCKSKIN SHIRT

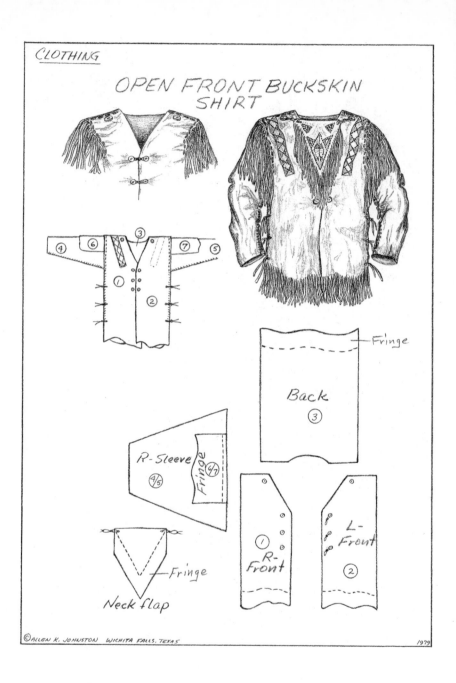

Fringe

Back
③

R-Sleeve
④/⑤

Fringe
④/⑦

Neck flap

Fringe

R-Front
①

L-Front
②

©ALLEN K. JOHNSTON   WICHITA FALLS, TEXAS   1979

PLATE 31

90

It was tough and durable, served as a wind breaker, and helped to provide concealment in the forest. The style and cut of the hunting shirt was similar to the tunic front long shirt as it was usually made at home by the women of the family.

The wilderness pilgrim wore full buckskins. Cloth was scarce and, although more comfortable and lighter than skins, was impractical for wilderness wear. Buckskins resisted briars and snags and stood up well under constant, hard wear. As cloth garments brought from civilization wore out, skin clothing was fashioned by the wearer using nothing for a pattern but the rags he was replacing. Buckskins took on varied patterns as their makers improved and simplified designs. Long fringe streamers danced and whipped as the pilgrim walked, keeping the insects stirred up and off of him. The fringe also served to soften the outline of a man and make him blend into the forest background. Added camouflage was gained by dying and marking the buckskins.

As the cultures of the white man and Indian blended, so did the style of dress. Paint and bead-decorated buckskins were quickly adopted by the mountain man and plainsman. The Indian decorated his ceremonial clothing to reflect his deeds, accomplishments, and social standing in the tribe. The white man was expected to make some show of social status among his people, whether he had any or not. He decorated his buckskins to elevate his standing and gain respect and acceptance among the Indians. The trick was to retain that respect and acceptance. It could have been fatal to lose it.

As winter winds blew cold, furs and blankets were added to the way of dress. A blanket was cut into body, sleeves, and hood which were sewn or laced together to make the capote. Buttons and toggles made of wood, bone, or horn, along with a wrap around tie sash of blanket material, served to keep the front of the capote closed. The plainsman made his winter wrap from the long haired neck and shoulder section of buffalo hides. The buffalo robe was heavy but it was warm and windproof. Mountain men made similar robes from bear skins.

Fur hats and caps were nothing more than large open pouches which fit over the head, ears, and neck. The hat was made from pelts or fur and were often fur-lined for added warmth. Mitts, or loose fitting fur bags were worn to cover the hands. Sometimes the

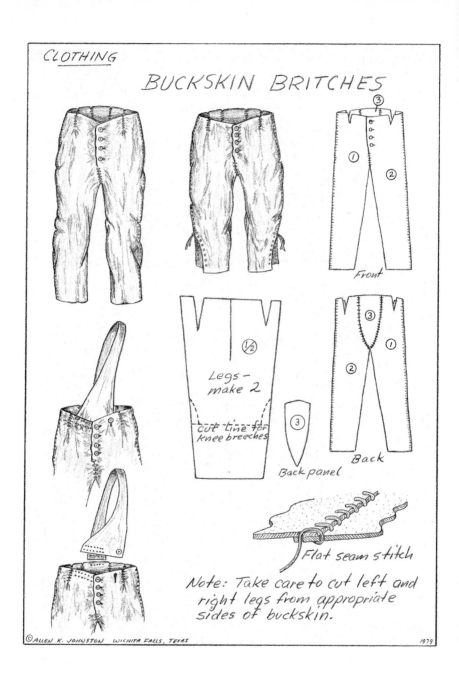

CLOTHING

BUCKSKIN BRITCHES

Front

Legs—
make 2

cut line for
knee breeches

Back panel

Back

Flat seam stitch

Note: Take care to cut left and
right legs from appropriate
sides of buckskin.

© ALLEN K. JOHNSTON   WICHITA FALLS, TEXAS   1979

PLATE 32

92

maker went to the trouble to separate the thumb from the mitten hand. A fur-lined pouch or muff, open at both ends and lined with rabbit fur, hung against the mountain man's chest. The muff provided hand protection from the numbing cold but left them free and ready for instant use. Scarves and mufflers made from blankets or pelts were worn around the neck and drawn across the chest.

Knitted cotton and wool stockings wore out in the wilderness and, when there were no more replacements, boots and moccasins were worn without socks. As snow and ice began to cover the ground, heavy strips of wool blanket material or fur were wrapped over the feet and up the legs. If the pilgrim could make it through the winter, he was confident that he could live for one more year.

In the settlements, the men usually had a choice of underclothing. Bleached cotton or linen knee-length drawers and lightweight undershirt, or long flannel drawers and shirt were the usual selections. The long flannels were commonly one-piece suits which eliminated the discomfort and bother caused by the drawers slipping down. In the wilderness, when flannels wore out, a breechcloth was made from some salvaged cloth remnants of worn out garments. When there was no more cloth, buckskin was even used for underwear.

The garments worn by the people of the 1700s to the 1850s were all hand sewn. Whether the clothing was made in the mills of England, France, America, or in the frontier cabin; hand stitching was the only way garments could be put together. Machine sewn clothing did not exist except for a few suits on exhibition in 1846. Elias Howe was granted a patent for the first practical sewing machine in that year and demonstrated it by machine sewing his own suits. The garment industry did not beat a path to Howe's door, in fact there wasn't a market for sewing machines until 1853.

Singer, and others who had pirated Howe's patent, began to establish a very small market for the new machines about 1853. Howe essentially shut down the industry through the courts until he was awarded a judgement and damages for patent infringements. The court battle lasted five years. Probably fewer than a hundred sewing machines were in use in the world by 1857. It took the tremendous production demands of the Civil War to establish the sewing machine in American industry.

A BUCKSKIN TUNIC

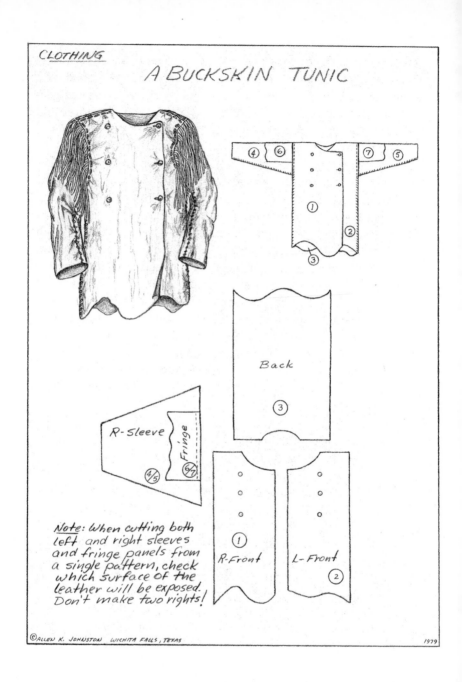

Back ③

R-Sleeve   Fringe ④/⑤ ⑥/⑦

Note: When cutting both left and right sleeves and fringe panels from a single pattern, check which surface of the leather will be exposed. Don't make two rights!

R-Front ①   L-Front ②

©ALLEN K. JOHNSTON   WICHITA FALLS, TEXAS   1979

PLATE 33

CLOTHING

FLAP FRONT BRITCHES

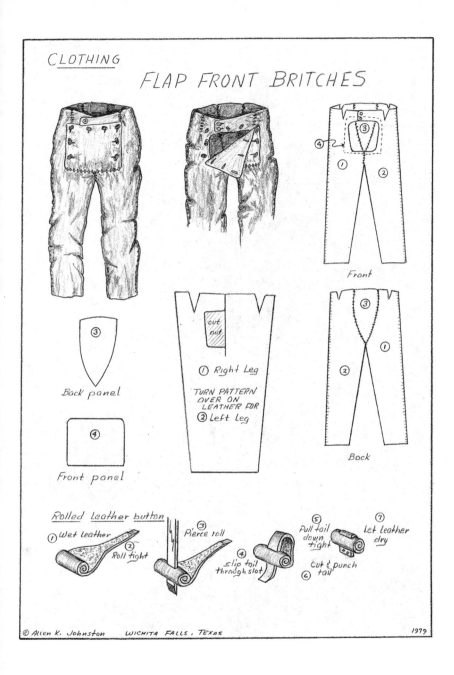

Back panel

Front panel

③

④ Right Leg

TURN PATTERN OVER ON LEATHER FOR
② Left Leg

cut out

Front

Back

Rolled leather button

① Wet leather
② Roll tight
③ Pierce roll
④ Slip tail through slot
⑤ Pull tail down tight
⑥ Cut & punch tail
⑦ Let leather dry

© Allen K. Johnston   WICHITA FALLS, TEXAS   1979

PLATE 34

95

WINTER COATS

Capote

Capuchin

1979

PLATE 35

Tools

Nothing is so frustrating as to start a job or project and find that a special tool is needed before the work can be completed. Many times, the difference between an artistically finished project and one that has been butchered is in the tools used on that project. My grandfather taught me that there is a job for every tool, and a tool for every job. This concept has caused me to load my tool cabinet with many tools over the years, but I still have to tool-up for special projects.

Next time you start a powder horn and want a scraper to work the inside of the horn, just try to find a horn scraper in the local hardware store. They are about as hard to find as hide scrapers and crook knives. The only way out of this dilemma is to make what you need.

The basic equipment for tool making includes: a bench grinder with both coarse and fine wheels; a torch to provide high temperatures for bending, annealing, and tempering; and an assortment of files and stones for shaping and finishing. Metals for tool making are easily obtained and include: old files; saw blades; flat springs; broken and worn cutting tools; and drill bits. Handles are easily made from wood, bone, or antler using epoxy cement to bond tools to handles.

Many special tools will be used only one time and never used again. Don't throw a tool away, someday it will be just right to rework into a sorely needed tool to do another special task. A small bin or tray on a shelf under the workbench makes an ideal cache for odds and ends of high grade steel for your tool making industry.

Most of the hand tools needed can be made by bending a piece of steel to an appropriate angle and sharpening an edge. A cutting head and shank made in one piece eliminates welding and brazing.

TOOLS

Knife blade

Files are a ready source
of high grade steel for
making cutting tools
and other items. Blades
made from files are
hard and hold an edge
well but are brittle.

Patch knife - razor ground

Scraper for working wood or horn

Flint striker

Ferriers hoof knife

Awl

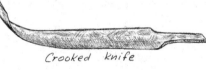
Crooked knife

Draw knife

Cross sections of common metal files

PLATE 36

Most of the common tool steels can be tempered to a useful hardness by heating to bright cherry red and quenching in motor oil. There are many methods of tempering steel and it would take several volumes to discuss them. If the needs of a particular job are beyond the simple tempering suggested above, I suggest that you research metallurgical processes in the public library.

A close friend, who has a background in Latin and who shares many of my interests, found a tempering process in a book in the rare books section of the University of Texas at Austin library. The book was written in Latin during the fifteenth century. I never knew the title of the book but I'll never forget the process. The blades of fine swords of the day were tempered in urine, and the better blades were tempered in the urine of priests and bishops. The finest blades, however, were quenched in the urine of a wine-drinking bishop. See? It just depends on how far you are willing to go to do a job right.

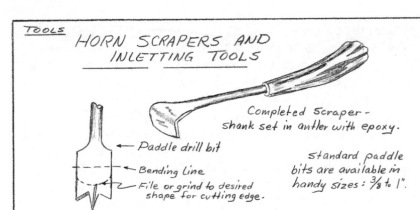

HORN SCRAPERS AND
INLETTING TOOLS

Completed Scraper - shank set in antler with epoxy.

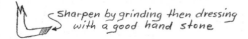

← Paddle drill bit

← Bending Line

← File or grind to desired shape for cutting edge.

Standard paddle bits are available in handy sizes : $\frac{3}{8}$ to 1".

Sharpen by grinding then dressing with a good hand stone

Cutting Paddle Drill Bits : Polish blade then heat with open gas flame. Watch for color changes in metal. Bands of blue, yellow, and red will appear followed by a dull gray color. Remove bit from heat when gray color appears — Let cool slowly. Blade is now soft enough to cut with file or hacksaw.

Bending and tempering blade : Heat blade to a bright cherry red, wedge between hardwood blocks, and quickly bend to 90° angle with shank. Reheat to bright cherry red and quench in oil to restore hardness.

© Allen K. Johnston   Wichita Falls, Texas   1979

PLATE 37

Shelter

Wilderness shelter covered a broad range of structures, both natural and man made. The wilderness provided erosional overhangs of rock, tree roots, and dirt embankments as well as caves, crevasses, and thick tangles of undergrowth for protection for animals and man from the ravages of the weather, and from each other. Man, being the least hardy of all animals, has always been able to compensate for his vulnerability to the elements and wild animals by building appropriate shelters.

Log cabins, rock or sod houses, and dugouts provided the best long term shelters with the protection and security of a fort. This type of structure was typical of the white man who brought the civilization concept into the wilderness. Trappers, hunters, and traders learned quickly to adapt the Indian style of living to their needs. It was far more sensible to put together a temporary shelter, if the anticipated weather required it, than to tie themselves to any one area with a cabin.

The lodges of the Indians were suitable for long term living in one place, but could be quickly dismantled and transported great distances. Small hunting parties seldom took lodges with them, but constructed simple lean-tos for the short term encampment. Animal hides were used as shelter covers and were heavy, and were transported on drags or travois. The white man brought canvas to the wilderness and created great trade opportunities.

Canvas shelters took many forms but the most popular was the simple canvas sheet. It could be set up in many shapes, depending on availability of poles and tie-offs, or used as a ground cloth and cover. When the canvas sheet was folded or rolled for transport, it was unnecessary to take the poles along, as with the tepee.

The canvas shelter in Plate 38 is very versatile and can be set

A VERSATILE CAMP TENT

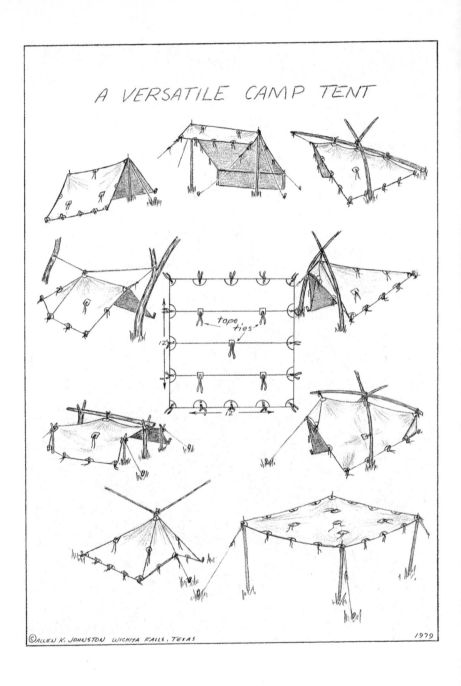

tape ties

©ALLEN K. JOHNSTON WICHITA FALLS, TEXAS

1979

PLATE 38

up in many forms. I made one like it some thirty years ago and used it for many, many outings. It was dyed to blend with the surroundings and served as a duck blind as well as a camp shelter. We were always careful to note the location of our camp because it generally faded into the background when it was set up as a formless lean-to. The material used in this particular shelter was a heavy muslin which was waterproofed with a homemade paraffin mixture that made it about as fire resistant as black gunpowder. I strongly recommend that you use our more modern waterproofing compounds which are flame retardant.

The Lodge Lounge

Primitive camping is the most enjoyable way to live in the outdoors. It requires minimum equipment and reduces problems of cargo space and transportation. It is, however, the least used method of camping because of the common notion that primitive camping has to be miserable. What does it take to make a camp comfortable? It takes adequate shelter, good food, a comfortable bed, and a place to relax. The short term camp of one or two days does not develop into the home-away-from-home that the ten day or two week camp does.

Camp improvements revolve around the two most important tools in the wilderness, the pocketknife and the hatchet or hand ax. These are the tools of the "Jackknife Industry." Pot hooks, forks, spoons, skewers, tent pegs, and other items of convenience are produced as needed. Woven mats for beds, shelter floors, privacy curtains, mattresses, sun shades, and lounges are comfort items easily manufactured from natural materials in the industry.

The Lodge Lounge is a simple woven mat supported by a tripod which is generally set firmly into the ground. The tripod holds about half of the mat up forming a comfortable back rest. Thin narrow slats made from reeds, split cane, or wood splints woven together with either jute cord or binder twine makes up the mat. Excellent woods for the project include willow, ash, and white oak. These materials split easily when they are freshly cut and green. A thin bladed knife and a tapping stick are all that's needed to make suitable slats. The lounge and loom for weaving the mat are illustrated in Plate 39.

The same primitive loom can be used to weave straw or grass mattresses. Colorful mats brighten up the camp. Dye the wood splints in several different colors and weave yourself a rainbow.

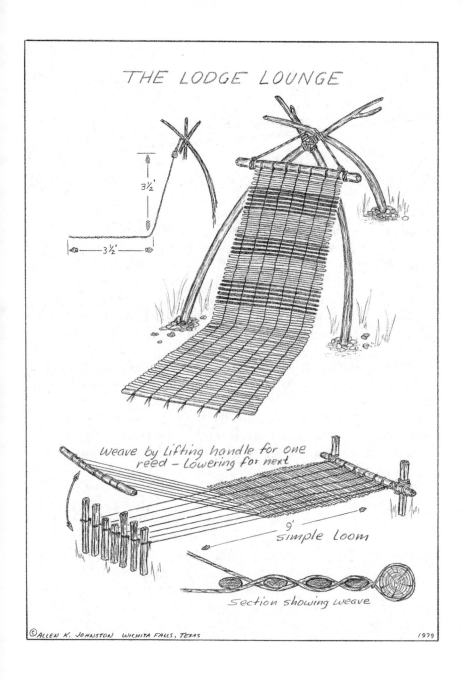

THE LODGE LOUNGE

3½'

3½'

Weave by lifting handle for one
reed - lowering for next

9'
simple loom

Section showing weave

© ALLEN K. JOHNSTON WICHITA FALLS, TEXAS   1979

PLATE 39

Pack Frames

We visualize the mountain man as making his way through the wilderness in his buckskins with powder horn and possible bag hanging at his side. His hands are empty except for his faithful long rifle. We picture the trapper paddling downstream in his canoe loaded with furs, dressed in a buckskin shirt with a red knit cap set jauntily on his head, as he makes his way to the buyer at the fort. Nobody ever seems to visualize these men loaded down like pack-horses carrying supplies, pelts, and traps as well as the canoe and paddle.

Transporting supplies into the wilderness for the season's trapping and trading business consumed much time and energy. White men used a cloth bag with shoulder, waist, and head harness to carry his impediments. Some of the journals from early expeditions describe these as great sacks, heavily loaded with goods and supplies. Big, strong voyageurs, playfully competing among themselves to see who was the strongest, made portages carrying the great sack, several bales of pelts, rifles, and canoes in a single load; as they raced each other downstream to civilization. Some of the loads carried were reported to be several hundred pounds.

Someone, sometime found that a wood frame with a harness to attach it to his back could be loaded with greater weight and balanced so that it carried easier and in greater comfort than the cloth packs. Nobody knows how far back in history the pack frame goes, but people have been rediscovering the pack frame for centuries. Indian squaws used an A frame before the white man came to this continent, and it is still being used in the wilds of Mexico and Central America. There is little doubt that the mountain men, plainsmen, trappers, and hunters adapted the wood frame to their needs at one time or another during the 1700s and 1800s.

TRAPPER'S PACK FRAME

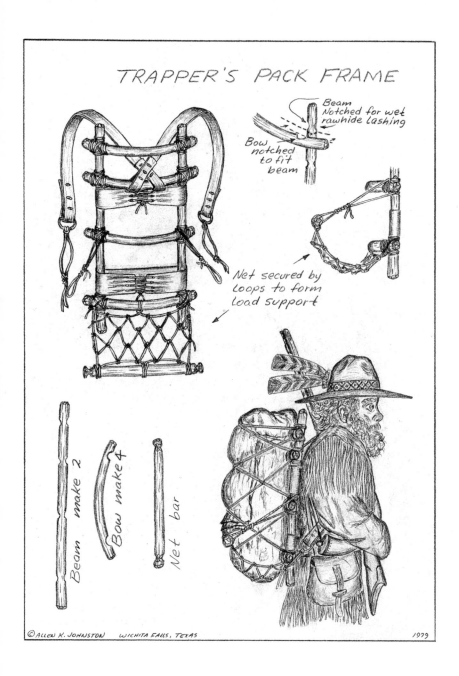

Beam Notched for wet rawhide lashing

Bow notched to fit beam

Net secured by loops to form load support

Beam make 2

Bow make 4

Net bar

© ALLEN K. JOHNSTON   WICHITA FALLS, TEXAS

1979

PLATE 40

107

Fire Making with Flint and Steel

The first friction matches were "Congreves" made in England in 1827. They were wood or cardboard strips dipped in sulfur and tipped with a mixture of potassium chlorate and antimony sulfide in mucilage. Matches made their appearance in America a year or so after they were invented. Friction matches, however, were considered luxury items and their cost, three matches for a penny, was thought prohibitive. Fires were started with flint and steel well into the 1880s.

Every early American household kept a tinder box with flint and steel on the mantle shelf to start home fires. Pocket tinder boxes went with every man into the wilderness. Fire was a key to survival rather than a mere convenience. Once a fire was started, it was carefully maintained day and night for as long as it was needed.

Thin wood splints were used to transfer a light from the fireplace to a candle or a smoking pipe. In the home, a stand of splints was kept on the shelf beside the tinder box. Sometimes spunks were kept with the wood splints. Spunks were sulfur tipped wood splints made by dipping splints into molten sulfur which cooled and hardened quickly. These durable and easily stored fire starters were readily ignited, burned with a hot flame, and retained it well. Spunks were used to transfer fire from tinder to wood chips in the fireplace. Small sulfur tipped splints were probably carried in pocket tinder boxes in the wilderness. An extra hot and long lasting flame made the spunk a good selection for winter emergencies. Still, the spunk had to be lighted with flint, steel, and tinder.

Fire making with flint and steel is almost as easy as making fire with friction matches. Irrespective of the method of ignition, the key to successful fire building is preparation. With flint and steel ignition, preparation begins with the assembly of the components of the fire making kit. Every item must be carefully selected, from steel to tinder box.

The steel should be of good carbon steel. An old flat file makes an excellent steel. Remove the teeth from the file and finish the metal to the smoothest possible surface with a grindstone. It seems that a smooth surface strikes the best spark. Keep the steel clean and rust free.

Carefully select the flints that are to be carried in the kit. Collect several pieces of flint and try them some evening or in the darkness of the garage or workshop to see which pieces appear to make the best sparks. There are several varieties of flint and some varieties strike better sparks than others.

Use either linen or cotton cloth to make the charred cloth, called punk, to catch the sparks. Linen is best but it is hard to find and cotton works nearly as well. Be sure that the cloth is 100 percent natural linen or cotton fiber. Synthetics and polyester blends just don't work. Cut the cloth into two inch squares and place them into a shallow metal container. Cover the container and set it over a burner on the cook stove. Let the cloth squares "cook" until smoke comes out from under the cover then remove the container from the heat and let it cool. Inspect the cloth to see that it has burned black but that it will still hold together when it is handled.

Tinder is defined as being any fine material that is highly flammable. There are many plants that put out fine, hair-like growths associated with flowers and seed heads, and other plants that have fibrous bark that burns well. A combination of fine, hair-like seed heads from common grasses and the bark stripped from dead, dry cedar limbs make very good tinder. Gather tinder whenever it is available and carefully dry and package it for future use. Any material selected for tinder should be dried then tested with a flame to see if it will burn with a blaze or smolder. Tinder has to blaze readily or it is worthless.

The container selected to be used for a tinder box should protect the tinder and charred cloth from moisture, though it need not be waterproof. The box should have a tight fitting lid and be large enough to hold flints, charred cloth, and enough tinder to

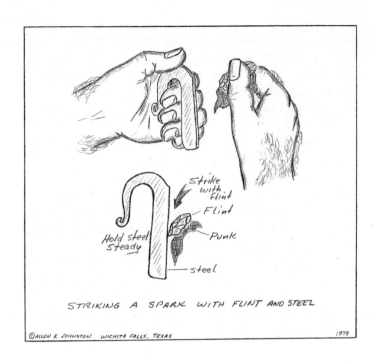

STRIKING A SPARK WITH FLINT AND STEEL

Strike with flint

Flint

Punk

Hold steel Steady

steel

PLATE 41

start several fires. The steel can be carried in the pouch or pocket. Tobacco cans, typewriter ribbon cans, and 16 mm film cans all make good tinder boxes. Replica tinder boxes of the 1700s are sold by various dealers of accouterments. A folded oilskin pouch also makes an excellent tinder box and is as authentic as the replicas.

Making a fire with flint and steel is a simple process. Take out a pinch of tinder and wad it into a bird nest. Experience will tell you how much tinder to use but for the first try, use enough to make a bird nest about the size of a walnut. Put the tinder in easy reach then select a flint and a piece of charred cloth. Hold the flint and charred cloth between the thumb and forefinger with the flint under the thumb, cloth at the bottom. The cloth should be positioned so that it will strike the steel with the flint but will not interfere with full contact of the flint on steel. Grasp the steel in the other hand being careful to keep the finger clear of the strike zone. Use a sharp broken edge of flint. Strike with a quick downward motion as though trying to chop a piece out of the steel with the stone. Strike the steel and check the cloth for a spark. When the cloth begins to burn, put down the steel and flint and pick up the bird nest. Carefully fold the smoldering part of the cloth into the tinder, blowing gently with the mouth to provide an air current to coax the material into a blaze. As soon as a blaze is established, quickly place the tinder into the fine kindling of the fire lay and get out the coffee pot. It won't be long until the fire is ready.

Starting fire by flint and steel takes practice but it can be done quickly and efficiently, once you get the hang of it. Basically, striking steel with flint produces tiny particles of hotly burning steel. When one of these burning particles catches in the charred cloth, ignition is established. The most important point to remember is to keep the cloth as close to the striking point of the spark as possible. See Plate 41. The farther a spark has to travel to reach the cloth, the smaller the burning particle becomes so that the remaining burn time is too short to maintain sufficient heat for ignition. The most common mistake is to put the cloth and tinder together on the ground and try to drop a spark into them from several inches above. You will become a successful flint and steel fire starter if you learn to do all of the work of gaining ignition in your hands.

The Bow and Arrow

Native Americans killed game for food and fought each other with clubs, throwing sticks, bows and arrows, darts, and spears long before the white man came to this continent. Blades for cutting tools were made from broken and chipped stone, sharply pointed pieces of bone, sharpened fragments of clam shells, thorns, and fire tempered pieces of hardwood. Metal technology was also present. The Aztec and Mayan People of what is now Mexico, the states of Arizona and New Mexico, knew how to work gold, silver and copper. Another copper-working culture existed among the Indians of the Northwest, Washington and Oregon.

The coming of the Spanish Conquistadors brought tools and weapons of iron and steel and new technology to North America. The presence of the new implements touched and affected the lives of comparatively few of the inhabitants of the North American Continent. Some of the new technology, like the few loose horses, began to grow and spread over the country. Tools and weapons, and a few pieces of armor, fell into the hands of the primitive people who made use of them as best they could. Nearly one hundred years after the arrival of the Conquistadors, colonization and exploration got underway in eastern North America. This time, trade tools and implements were made available to the Indians in the hope of cultivating friendship and trust. The people saw axes, hatchets, knives, and many other useful implements made of iron and steel for the first time. The tool trade for food and furs placed a white man's hatchet into the hand of an Indian and thus was born the tomahawk.

Bows and arrows were nothing new to the white man as the English bowmen were expert with the longbow well before The Battle of Hastings in the year 1066. Europeans were introduced to the short bow during the Crusades in the thirteenth century when they fought against the Turks. The crossbow was, and still is, a classic of power and accuracy. Long before the firearm was any more than a curiosity, the crossbow was considered to be the ultimate weapon and steps were taken to outlaw or control its use by leaders throughout Europe. European settlers colonizing this country were historically close enough to the time of the common use of the longbow to appreciate its usefulness. There is little doubt that a few colonials used the arrow to harvest game from the forest.

Trappers and fur traders penetrated deeper and deeper into the wilderness of America, and traded literally thousands of weapons in the form of metal arrow points, hatchets, tomahawks, and knives for prime pelts. White men ventured hundreds of miles from settled areas to live for many months at a time as they trapped and traded for beaver furs. Supplies for the extended expeditions created problems. Among the problems were supplies of powder and lead. Powder was light in weight and could be taken into the wilderness in relatively large quantities, but lead was heavy and there was a practical limit to how much a man could carry. During this period, lead was so valuable on the frontier that it was used in place of coins and currency. In the wilderness, it was worth a man's life.

A mountain man depended on his excellence at weapons to survive. Knowing the limits of the long rifle, it was necessary for him to develop skills with the knife and tomahawk. Adding the use of the spear and the bow and arrow were natural steps toward rounding out his weapons inventory and conserving powder and lead. Living among the Indians as he did; it would have been difficult, if not dangerous, to refuse to participate in friendly games at weapons with his hosts; the bow and arrow, as well as the spear and dart, became familiar and useful. Sometime during the 1700s, the white man must have exerted his influence on the Indian bow. Out of several authenticated and dated bows from the Great Lakes region, some specimens have handle risers amazingly similar and typical of the European longbow.

Making a serviceable bow is not as hard as it might seem, the first part of the job is psychological. There are many laminated, fiberglass, stabilized, working recurve bows on the market today.

THE BOW AND ARROW

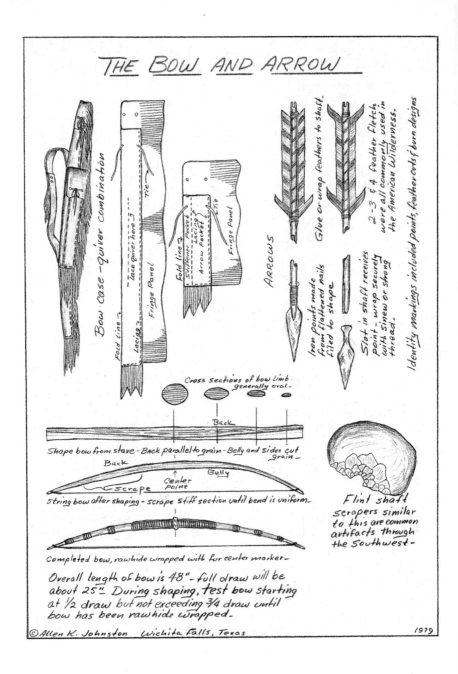

Bow case-quiver combination

Fold line
Lacing
Fringe Panel
Lace quiver here
Tie
Fringe Panel

Fold line
Stiffener Pocket
Lacing
Arrow Pocket
Tie
Fringe Panel

ARROWS

Glue or wrap feathers to shaft.

2-3 & 4 feather fletch were all commonly used in the American Wilderness.

Identity markings included points, feather cuts & burn designs.

Iron points made from flattened nails filed to shape.

Slot in shaft receives point - wrap securely with sinew or strong thread.

Cross sections of bow limb generally oval

Back

Shape bow from stave - Back parallel to grain - Belly and sides cut grain.

Back
Belly
Scrape
Center Point

String bow after shaping - scrape stiff section until bend is uniform.

Completed bow, rawhide wrapped with fur center marker.

Flint shaft scrapers similar to this are common artifacts through the Southwest.

Overall length of bow is 48" - full draw will be about 25". During shaping, test bow starting at ½ draw but not exceeding ¾ draw until bow has been rawhide wrapped.

© Allen K. Johnston   Wichita Falls, Texas

1979

PLATE 42

114

There are also several makes of compound bows with wheels, pulleys, cables, and spring steel limbs that bear little resemblance to a bow except that they cast arrows. These fine bows shoot great distances with comparative ease and accuracy, and are made of beautiful exotic materials. The idea of making a bow that will compete with these wonders of modern technology is unthinkable. Well, not quite, for several reasons.

The Indian bow of the 1700 to 1800 period was crude, being made from native materials of questionable resiliency by the use of stone tools. It was reinforced by the use of sinew or rawhide and was strung with a string of animal intestine, sinew, plant fiber, or a combination of the three. The bow, depending on the wood and its shaping, ranged from stiff and heavy to a light and willowy draw and had limited cast. These bows were not much by the archery standards of today. In fact, the Indians would have been outclassed had the first settlers arrived with nothing but English longbows. Game animals, however, were not so wary and the stalking ability of the Indian offset the need for long shots. Deep penetration in thick skinned game, bear and buffalo, was gained by using very small, sharp points at close range and high velocity. Collectors call these tiny arrowheads "bird points." Realistically, it is easier to gain deep penetration through thick, tough hide and massive muscle with an ice pick than it is with a broom handle.

The next hurdle to overcome is to find suitable material to make a bow. Wood bow staves are still available from a few of the older archery equipment dealers. Native materials such as osage orange, hemlock, hickory, oak, ash, and gum are all useable woods. If a ready curved stave is not available, one will have to be cut and cured before the project can proceed. Select a reasonably straight limb that is about three inches in diameter and long enough to make a 48 inch bow. Split the limb into a round stave about $1\frac{1}{2}$ inches in diameter, following the wood grain and removing the sap wood. Paint the cut ends with any oil base paint to seal them and store the stave in a dry, dark place to cure. It would be best to cure several staves at the same time so that you can make more than one bow. Curing time for the wood will be about six months, depending on the density of the wood and the climate of your area, so plan ahead.

Absolute straightness of the limb is not too important as few of the Indian made bows were more than reasonably straight. The straightness of a limb depended on the run of the wood grain. This is the important thing to bear in mind while shaping the bow, the run of the grain. Try to keep the back of the bow parallel to the grain of the wood and use the natural curvature of the limb to your advantage. Taper the bow from the belly and sides, cutting grain as the taper develops. The grain in the bow back must not be cut. Shape the limb round in the center section, progressing to oval then flattened oval toward the ends. This type of bow flexes over the entire length, while the typical longbow is stiff in the center section and works at both ends. The full flex design allows the short bow to achieve full draw without wasted length. Remember too, the Indians did not use the classic archer's draw but shot from whatever draw their bows would stand.

After your bow has been shaped to the desired form, string the bow to a normal curve and check the curvature of the limb. If it bends more at one end than at the other, scrape the belly of the bow in the area where more bend is needed to distribute the curvature evenly. Flex the bow to half draw and check for both curvature and weight of pull. Repeat this procedure for three-quarter draw but do not pull beyond this point until the rawhide wraps are in place and thoroughly dry. At half draw the pull should not exceed 15 pounds, at three-quarters draw it should not exceed 25 pounds. If the pull exceeds the desired weights, scrape the bow to remove enough wood to lower the weight. The finished bow should be in the 25 to 35 pound pull range. The weight of pull does not necessarily indicate the bow's power. A cable on a short length of a utility pole may have a 1,980 pound pull at 26 inch draw but that doesn't mean it will shoot a shaft 700 yards. It is limb action, not pull weight, that delivers cast to an arrow.

With the scraping and flexing operations completed, the bow is ready for a coat of varnish to seal the wood and prolong its life. Wait until the varnish is completely dry, then wrap the bow tightly with wet rawhide. Wrap the center section first, winding eight inches each side of the center point of the limb. Wrap the rest of the bow with evenly spaced wraps of about ten windings each. Let the rawhide dry for several days then varnish the bow again, soaking the hide windings heavily with varnish. The final touch is to locate the center point of the bow and mark it with a narrow band of fur wrapped around the limb. The bow is ready to use.

Make a bow string out of waxed linen thread, doubling the thread until the thickness of the string is about one-eighth inch. Wax the string heavily then twist it together and wax again. Beeswax is the only wax to use. You may want to use dacron thread or a commercial bow string, these are available from one of the archery supply companies. Arrow shafts and turkey feathers are also available. Metal points are easy to make by beating large nails flat and filing to shape. The Indians became very proficient at making hammered iron points out of nails gathered after a cabin roast during the 1800s.

Carrying the bow and arrow is easy with a rig made like the Indians made them. The one shown in Plate 42, was reconstructed from an existing case-quiver combination in a private collection. The rig with its bow and three arrows were found in an exceptional state of preservation under several inches of compacted dirt in the floor of a cave in New Mexico. Note that the quiver is divided into two sections, one for the arrows and the other for a stick to stiffen the quiver to protect the arrows. The stick is sewn in and is an integral part of the case-quiver combination.

The completed rig goes well with a set of mountain man skins. With a little practice, a great deal of fun and enjoyment can be had shooting arrows through a rolling hoop or shooting the mark in a rendezvous contest at weapons.

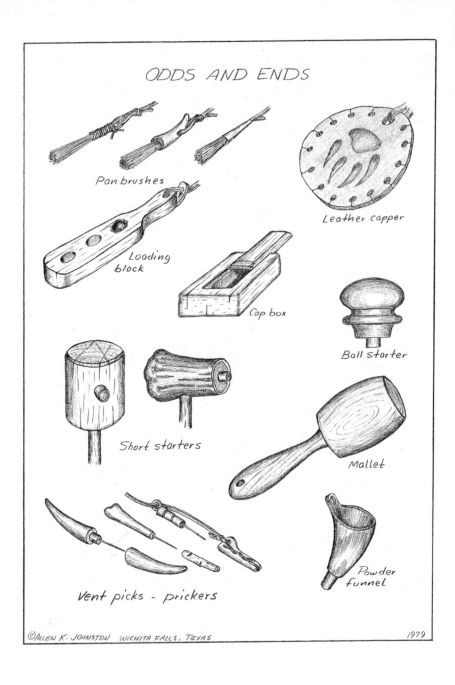

ODDS AND ENDS

Pan brushes

Leather capper

Loading block

Cap box

Ball starter

Short starters

Mallet

Vent picks - prickers

Powder funnel

©Allen K. Johnston   Wichita Falls, Texas

1979

Plate 43

118

Cooking

One key to successful camping, as mentioned before, is good food. This poses no problem because anything that can be prepared at home in the kitchen can be prepared over the campfire. The principle difference is convenience. Forethought and preparation can overcome the difference, making every outing a success. Basically, there are four methods of cooking: frying, baking, broiling, and boiling. All foods are prepared by these methods whether alone or in combination. Frying requires a vessel containing hot grease which may be drained off at the appropriate stage of cooking and replaced with water, wine, or special sauce and covered to simmer until the food is done. Baking is done in a container which maintains a desired heat evenly distributed around the food being cooked. Broiling is exposing the food to a high heat on one side at a time and may be done on a gridiron, directly over a bed of coals, or on a grill or dry skillet. Boiling is cooking by immersing food in hot water until it is tender or edible. These four methods are no different in the ultramodern kitchen, only the appliances differ.

The first consideration for outdoor cooking is the available fuel that will be used to provide heat. If the fuel is wood, remember that pine burns very quickly and does not produce coals. It also imparts a turpentine taste to food broiled over the flames as well as leaving a heavy coating of black soot on cooking vessels. Hardwoods, mesquite, oak, hickory, etc., produce coals that put out even, strong heat and have a pleasant aroma and taste to the smoke. Buffalo or cow chips smoulder, put off considerable smoke, and taste and smell like hell. By considering the type of fuel that will be available to the camp, it will be easy to prepare a menu and select the utensils that will be needed. If gasoline or propane fuel is to be used, the manufacturers of the stoves offer a broad selec-

119

tion of accessories for baking, toasting, and general cooking. This is not quite mountain man style, but in today's hurry world it may be the way for some of our twentieth century pilgrims to go.

The second consideration is transportation. It would be poor judgement to backpack a twelve inch cast iron kettle and a lid into some remote wilderness area unless the plan was to establish a long term camp. On the other hand, an assortment of cast iron ware is most welcome in a camp when transportation is by automobile or wagon. The pioneer family moving west carried as complete an assortment of cooking ware as they could assemble, giving this priority over frills and conveniences. They knew the importance of eating well to stay healthy and strong. The Indians ate differently so that their cooking methods were very simple. In this section, I will describe some of the primitive methods of food preparation and also put together some recipes for the camp.

Cooking Underground

One of the earlier methods of cooking used in the southwestern United States was baking food in a pit dug into the ground. The pulpy root of the sotol plant, one of the dagger-leafed succulents growing in the semiarid Southwest, was cooked in pits by the native inhabitants. Carbon dating of charcoal samples taken from some of the pits unearthed during archeological investigations indicate that some of the older cookers were used 2,500 years ago. Many of these pits have been uncovered and they all follow the same pattern of construction. The pits measure about two feet deep and three to four feet across. They were bowl shaped and completely lined with flat rocks set in mud. The hard-baked clay under the rocks indicate that the inside of the pits were heated very hot before food was put in to cook. A few pits have been opened with food still in them. Putting all of the pieces together, it seems that once the pit was constructed, a hot fire was built in the hole and maintained for quite a while in order to heat the earth. When the right temperature was reached the ashes and coals were removed and the hole was filled with sotol stalk and root, then covered with

COOKING FIRES

Keyhole Fire

Large hot fire with lots of coals - shovel hot coals into cooking chanel for pots and pans or lift out for bake kettle -

Excellent general purpose camp cooking fire -

Star Fire

Long sticks pushed into burn area as they burn off. Good fire for light cooking. Small fire, few coals -

Indian Fire - sit close, keep warm -

Dakota Hole

Uses small sticks and twigs consumes fuel rapidly but burns like blast furnace - Excellent for quick pot of coffee or melting lead for casting rifle balls -

Reflector Fire

Rock or green log back reflects heat into baking oven or tent -

White man's fire - Burn face - freeze butt -

© Allen K. Johnston   WICHITA FALLS, TEXAS   1979

PLATE 44

121

a mat woven from the long supple leaves of the plant. The mat was covered with several inches of dirt and a roaring fire was then built over the pit. The fire could be maintained for several days until the cooking was considered adequate.

This method of baking works very well if you are not in a hurry. A large quantity of food will take longer by this method than a smaller pit with less food. The following was prepared to feed a party of thirty people:

2   turkeys (approximately 20 pounds each)
20   pounds white potatoes (whole, unpeeled)
10   pounds carrots (whole, unpeeled)
5   pounds apples (cut in half)
     salt
     pepper

The pit used for this quantity was about 2 feet deep and 3 feet across. It was unlined but cleaned of loose dirt. The pit was filled with wood and set afire and allowed to burn most of the night, about 6 hours. During the last half hour, the turkeys were salted and peppered well, inside and out; the potatoes and carrots washed, and the apples cut in half. The ashes, coals, and loose dirt were cleaned from the pit and a large square of clean, white cloth was spread out to form a liner for the hole. The turkeys were placed on their backs on top of the cloth then the apples put cut-side down on the birds. This was followed by the carrots, then the potatoes. The cloth was carefully folded over the food and the pit covered with canvas. Finally, about 4 inches of dirt covered everything. A large camp fire was built on top of the pit and maintained all of the next day and into the night. The fire was allowed to die out after the last pot of coffee when the camp turned in for the night. The food was left encased in the hot earth until afternoon of the next day when the rest of the gang arrived.

Maintaining the fires and waiting for the meal to finish cooking would have been a monotonous chore had it not been for the obliging nature of the fish in the lake by which we were camped. With the arrival of the gang, the pit was carefully opened and the dinner lifted out in the cloth cover. All of the food was still too hot to handle but it didn't slow that bunch down. The meal was a howling success.

Cooking on the Coals

Broiling or roasting food directly on the coals is as old as the use of fire. The gridiron, even though it has been around for hundreds of years, is a relative newcomer to cooking, considering the length of time man has cooked over coals. This is a method of cooking that has been almost overlooked by the modern-day outdoorsman. Try cooking with it, then consider its possibilities.

Roasting Ears

Build a large bed of coals and when the fire is almost gone, lay on several ears of corn in the shuck. After about 4 minutes, roll the corn and let the heat work on the other side for another 4 minutes, then remove the ears from the coals. Several layers of the outer shucks will be burned but the corn within will be sweet and tender. Remove the shucks and silks, butter, salt and pepper to taste, and wade in. Remember, if you find a worm, don't say anything; everyone else might want one too! When cooking roasting ears for a large party it helps to wear gloves and do the turning and lifting with a pitch fork. It also helps to use a large bed of coals, cooking corn on half of the bed while the fire and coals come back to life on the other half. The high moisture content of the ears produce considerable steam, cooling the coals rapidly and increasing cooking time proportionally.

Steak on the Coals

Here's one that you can try in your brazier in the back yard. Go first class on this one, its worth it. Select a well marbled prime sirloin steak about the size of a blacksmith's apron. Salt and pepper the meat to your liking and set it to one side. Build a fire in the brazier using hard wood chunks, not charcoal. Let the fire burn down to a bed of brightly glowing coals. Lay the meat directly on the coals and cook it to your fancy, anything from rare to well done. Turn the steak as it cooks and do not allow the coals to blaze up. It may take a sprinkle of water to keep the flames down. You will find that the meat will not stick to the coals or ashes and will be as clean as if cooked on a metal grill.

You say you don't believe it? Well, while you are trying to decide whether or not to sacrifice your steak, make a couple of cups of coffee to settle the nerves. Now that the coals are glowing bright red and the flames are gone, take a small brownpaper bag and put in about 3 cups of water. Set the bag of water on the coals and let it come to a boil, then put in 3 teaspoons of ground coffee and let it boil for a few moments, remove the sack from the heat and pour into cups. Wad the bag into a ball and throw it in the trash. Now if you can do that, you can sure cook a steak without burning it. Remember, no flames, let the coals do the cooking. No, there were no brown paper bags in the wilderness but there were birch bark buckets in the north woods that would behave the same way for boiling water.

Other Cooking Methods

Primitive cooking methods included roasting on sticks and spits, baking by radiated heat by propping meat or fish near a brightly burning fire, using hot rocks to boil food in a sack made of animal skin, and many other methods. Eating has always taken two avenues, eating for enjoyment and eating for survival. When it comes right down to the nitty-gritty of basic survival it becomes a serious business. Finding food is the main problem and once it is in hand, the hungry person will find a way to cook it. That's as it has been since the dawn of human existence.

Fortunately, we are not faced with the survival situation in our outdoor recreation, so cooking and eating can be enjoyable experiences. It is worthwhile, however, to become familiar with native foods available in the wilderness in case an outing meets with disaster. Food packs or cooking utensils can be lost from an overturned canoe, a flash flood, a landslide, forest fire, or some other unexpected situation. By learning and trying primitive and novel methods of preparing food, the camper will discover methods which serve his purpose well, and at the same time reduce the number and variety of cooking utensils needed for the next trip. The early mountain man, plainsman, and trader learned new foods and primitive methods to prepare what was available so that they were able to live indefinitely in the wilderness without need of skillet or kettle. Many of them deserted their civilized ways for the new life while others periodically returned to partake of the luxuries of rich food and strong drink. Often what they returned to was hardly worth the trip, early life was rough in the settlements too.

Food

The new nation suffered many growing pains, from the densely settled areas of the original colonies all the way to the westward moving frontier. Small farms produced what they could and had to put back a supply of food for the family in order to survive the winter. The surplus amounted to relatively little when taking into account the number of people that needed food. Every household had a small garden to supplement the available food supply. Fortunately, England subsidized the colonies until the revolution or things would have been far worse.

There were no supermarkets so the pioneer family ate what was ready in the field or garden. If the pumpkin crop was ready, they ate pumpkin. They may have preferred cabbage and potatoes but they ate pumpkin, not once, but meal after meal. It was served baked, stewed, boiled, roasted, made into breads, pies, and candy, or eaten raw. The same thing happened when it was potato time, and each time something else ripened. When winter came, they ate whatever was most likely to spoil first. Eating must have been the least enjoyed gathering of the day. Finding new ways to serve the same thing meal after meal must have been exasperating to the woman of the house as she continually experimented in order to keep the family eating.

Meat was in short supply in the more populated areas of the colonies after 1670 because nearly all of the game which had been so abundant had been wasted. The demand for the soft, supple buckskin for export had led to destruction of the forests as well as the game. Large circular fires were set in the forest to drive the deer together where they perished as the flames closed on them. The fires took everything; turkey, quail, grouse, squirrel, rabbit, bear...everything. Hides were stripped from the deer and the carcasses left to rot. The game that survived migrated away from the inhabited areas, leaving the people to depend on fish and water fowl to supplement limited supplies of beef and pork.

The meat situation on the frontier was much brighter. Wild game from the forest was abundant and easily harvested. They also supplemented the game with beef and pork, although beef was to be in very short supply for many more years. Field crops on the frontier had to be grains, root crops, and beans; crops that could stand storage and transportation to market. Garden vegetables were consumed by the family on the farm. Flax and cotton took up planting area by necessity. The frontiersman-farmer considered he had a prosperous year if he fed and clothed the family and turned a cash profit of $150 during the early 1700s.

The following sections deal with selected topics and recipes, many from the colonial period and some from later periods. Some of the recipes are delights, some are fair, and some are put in to show what the hungry pilgrim did to keep his backbone from rubbing blisters on his belly.

Bread

The modern American baking industry has just about ruined bread as a food. The super light, hand twisted, snow white, half raw packages of fluff being sold to the consumer are disgraceful to the established image of bread. Bread is no longer the staff of life... the only life that modern day bread is capable of supporting is mold.

European breads brought to this country by the early settlers were whole grain, heavy, dark breads. One slice of the heavy breads and a piece of cheese was all that was needed to make a satisfying lunch. That one slice provided flavor, body, and nutrition to satisfy the needs of the hungry pilgrim. Many of the grains used in the early breads are now apparently unfit for American consumption and are considered suitable only for livestock and poultry feeds and for export to foreign countries.

There were many breads used on the frontier. Some were no

more than flour, salt, and water (hard tack) while others were lighter and more flavorful.

Hard Tack

Hard tack, or ship's biscuit, has been around for more than two thousand years. This food has been carried and eaten as a field ration by every nation in the world. It was standard U.S. Army ration all the way up to 1941. Make up a small batch and pass it out to the youngsters of the neighborhood to broaden their education and give them a little appreciation of the hardships of the frontier and cattle drives. Jerky and hard tack made a small package but would sure go a long way... farther than a man's teeth, usually.

3   cups flour (unbleached white or whole wheat)
3   teaspoons salt

Mix the two together and add water, a little at a time, until a tough elastic dough has been formed. Dust the surface of a bread board with flour then roll the dough to a thickness of about $1/4$ inch. Cut into squares about 2 inches on the sides, lift off the board and place on a flat pan or cookie sheet. Punch holes through the dough with the tines of a fork, several holes in each square like a soda cracker. Bake at 350°F until the bread is browned. Don't expect the hard tack to rise and be crisp and tender like a cracker, it won't be.

Bannock

This is a pan bread that is easily put together at the camp fire.

2   cups whole wheat flour
3   teaspoons baking powder
$1/2$ teaspoon salt

Add $1/2$ cup (approximate measure) cold water and mix into dough then form into a ring, dust with whole wheat flour and place into a large cast iron skillet. Place on the coals and cook, move the skillet as needed to provide even heat, until the bottom of the ring is lightly browned. Prop the skillet near the fire using the highest possible angle, without the bread sliding out, and finish cooking by radiated heat until the top of the ring is light brown. Bannock cooks in 20 to 30 minutes when the fire is right.

Biscuits

The bake kettle, now almost universally called a dutch oven, is the most versatile cooking vessel in camp. It can be used to bake anything that can be baked at home in the oven. If you have never used one, try it. Cooking in one of these can be quickly mastered and will change a hum-drum camping vacation into one of culinary delight. If you are already familiar with this faithful camp companion, pass your talent on to a neighbor... he'll appreciate it, and it may improve his vacation too.

Prepare your bake kettle by wiping the inside with a clean cloth or paper towel. Place a single slice of bacon in the bottom, put the lid on the kettle and place it on the coals. This will serve to sterilize the vessel, grease the inside, and heat it up; all in one operation. Cook the bacon until it is useless as food, it will not matter if it burns.

While the kettle is on the coals, mix your biscuit dough.

2   cups flour (unbleached or whole wheat)
2   teaspoons baking powder
$1/2$ teaspoon salt

Mix the dry ingredients and cut in or blend:

3   tablespoons bacon grease or shortening

Then work in about 1 cup of water—milk if you wish—mixing to a dough. If you want to make drop biscuits, pinch off or spoon out portions of dough an inch and a half in diameter and drop them into the kettle (remove the bake kettle from the coals first). Arrange biscuits so that they are separated about an inch, so they brown evenly and do not cook together. Place the lid on the kettle and, with a shovel, remove a few coals from the fire and place them on the ground. Set the kettle on the coals and, again with the shovel, place 5 or 6 large glowing coals on top of the lid. Allow the bread to bake about 10 minutes then remove the lid and check to see that the bottoms of the biscuits are not burning, replace the cover and continue baking until the tops are lightly browned. Experience will soon teach you how few coals are needed to bake bread in the bake kettle. Cooking time for biscuits is usually about 20 minutes. When they come off of the fire, be sure to have plenty of butter and honey available and dig in.

BAKING AT THE OPEN FIRE

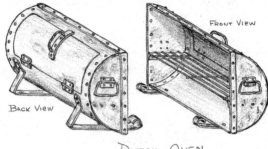

FRONT VIEW

BAKES BY RADIATED
AND REFLECTED HEAT.
ACCESS TO FOOD FROM
DOOR AT REAR —

EARLY AMERICAN AND
EUROPEAN —

PRE-1600 TO
PRESENT

BACK VIEW

DUTCH OVEN

BAKES BY RADIATED AND
REFLECTED HEAT. LIGHTER
AND MORE PORTABLE
THAN DUTCH OVEN —

FOOD ACCESS FROM
FRONT —

PRE - 1800 TO PRESENT

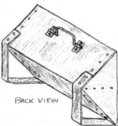

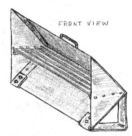

FRONT VIEW

BACK VIEW

REFLECTOR OVEN

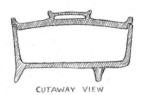

CUTAWAY VIEW

BAKES BY CONDUCTED HEAT FROM COALS
IN LID AND UNDER KETTLE - EARLY AMERICAN
AND EUROPEAN - PRE
1600 TO PRESENT.

BAKE KETTLE

PLATE 45

Biscuits can be baked in a skillet as described in the cooking of bannock, or in strips wound around a large diameter stick. The stick should be of a wood that has a pleasant taste. Peel the bark from a stick (about 2 inches in diameter) and wrap the last 10 to 12 inches of the stick with a strip of dough about $1/4$ inch thick by 1 inch wide. Spiral wind the dough, starting with a circular turn to anchor the dough, then finishing the wrap with another circular turn. Put the wrapped end of the stick over the hot coals and lightly brown the dough as quickly as possible to give strength to the bread and prevent it from breaking off and falling into the fire. Trial and error will give you experience and, though you will lose a few yards of perfectly good biscuits into the fire, you will eat far more than you will lose.

Cobblers

Cobblers are basically an expansion of the basic biscuit recipe. They are delightful desserts and the kids love them. Short breads are best when prepared with fresh, wild fruits and berries. Canned cherries, plumbs, blueberries, and the like are not so tantalizing as the fresh fruits, but when the time comes to open the bake kettle, the youngsters never complain about the can.

To the basic biscuit recipe add:

1   cup honey or sugar
2   tablespoons bacon grease or shortening (this is in addition to the 3 already used)

Stir sugar in when mixing the dry ingredients or mix in honey with $1/2$ cup water. Using about half of the dough, spread it over the bottom of the kettle forming a thickness of about $1/2$ inch and bringing the dough up the sides of the kettle about 2 inches. This makes a bowl shaped biscuit.

To the remaining dough, stir in the juice of one large can of pie cherries, then fold in the fruit. Scrape this into the bowl shaped dough liner in the kettle. Place the lid on the kettle and bake as for biscuits.

Freshly gathered fruits and berries will not provide the moisture that canned fruit does, so you will have to use more water when mixing fruit with the remaining dough. Tart or sour fruits need honey or sugar to bring them up to the liking of the young-

131

sters so use $1/2$ cup sugar mixed with tart fruits and 1 cup with sour fruits per each cup of fruit.

It takes a bit longer to bake a cobbler due to the thickness and added moisture so allow about 45 to 55 minutes cooking time. Be sure to check on the progress of the cooking to insure even cooking.

Yeast

Dry yeast was no stranger to the colonial or wilderness home. A supply of dry yeast was kept in nearly every home and was rejuvenated once or twice each year. There is baker's yeast and a brewer's, or winemaker's, yeast. Saccharomyces cerevisiae are the wee beasties responsible for the rising of bread and sourdough biscuits... and for the alcohol and carbon dioxide in beer and sparkling wines, as well as for the kick in moonshine. In the early days it was not possible to run down to the supermarket for a couple of packages of yeast, so yeast was propagated and maintained in each home. Original starts for yeast came from peddlers making the rounds of the frontier cabins and settlements carrying a small quantity of dry yeast. Starts came from a pinch of sourdough or a scrape of dry yeast. Anywhere beer was available, enough yeast could be had from a pint of beer to provide starts for every home in America. It may have been inconvenient to travel 3 or 4 days on foot to buy, beg, or borrow a start but it was a necessity.

A scrape of dry yeast was put into a crockery jar containing a quart of warm water, a pint of milk, a quarter of a cup of sugar and an egg; all well mixed together. The crock was placed near the hearth to stay warm and work overnight. The next day the jar was filled with a thick and foaming paste of sweet, fresh yeast. If the start was from beer, the jar contained only half a quart of water, but all of the other ingredients, to which the pint of beer was added, remained the same. Starting from a sourdough source was accomplished as with the dry yeast scrape.

Once the yeast was ready, bread was mixed and put on to bake, a wad of the dough was placed into a small crockery jar and covered with dry flour and a lid. This was the new sourdough starter. Some of the new yeast was prepared for drying. Still more

132

of the sweet, fresh yeast was mixed into a thin paste made of a mixture of milk, beaten eggs, sugar, and flour then covered with a clean cloth and left in a warm place near the hearth to bloom again. The next day, it was a fragrant container of foaming yeast.

While the yeast was working, a wood bowl was scraped, scoured, and carefully washed then set to one side to dry; upside down to keep the dust off of the clean surface. When the yeast was ready, a clean brush was used to paint the inside of the bowl with the frothing mixture. Again, the bowl was laid bottom-side-up to dry. Many coats of yeast were stored in the wood bowl, which was turned upside down in a cool, dry place so that the yeast would last for many months. From time to time a scrape of yeast would be taken from the bowl as needed for baking. The pot of sour dough usually served for most of the baking but if there was to be more baking done than usual, then the homemaker had to draw on her backup supply of yeast.

Beer Bread

Yeast bread is as easy to put together in camp as it is in the home kitchen. There is no deep, dark secret to making bread. In fact, once you understand the mechanics of bread making, you won't ever need a recipe again. Flour and salt mixed together does two things; first, salt flavors the flour, and second, salt acts as a carrier to help carry moisture into the flour and distribute it more evenly. When flour and water are mixed it forms a gluten, a thick and tough paste. When the yeasties go to work, they feed on nutrients in the flour and pass off alcohol and carbon dioxide gas as waste. Since the yeast cell is encased in the gluten, a gas bubble is formed. There are millions of yeast cells working at the same time with each rapidly reproducing itself, doubling and redoubling the number of working beasties. The result is that the bread rises as the gas bubbles expand. Now for the beer bread:

8   cups flour (white)
2   teaspoons salt
2   cans of your favorite beer (one warm, one cold)

Use a large pan and mix salt and flour together thoroughly. Open the warm can of beer and pour it into the flour-salt mixture, working it in as you go, making a smooth dough. There may not be enough beer to blend with the quantity of flour and a little additional moisture may be needed, add a small amount of water. When the dough is a smooth and elastic mass, divide it into three or four equal portions and roll into loaves. Dust the loaves with flour and set aside to rise. When they have doubled their size, put into the oven or bake kettle to bake. This bread is light with a tough, crisp crust... a French bread.

Ah, yes... the cold can of beer is for the cook.

Heavy Bread

This bread lives up to its name. The recipe makes up four loaves, weighing about two pounds each, with enough food value to supply a small army. The ingredients are available at the local market or at the local health food store. Use this recipe as written or change it to fit your own taste. Don't be afraid to experiment, if you want to use millet or grain sorghum... put in millet or grain sorghum. Remember, the pilgrim family used what they could find.

Using a two quart container, mix and beat together:

3   cups milk
1   cup raw honey
6   eggs

Stir in 1 package of dry yeast, cover the container with a clean cloth and set it in a warm place. Let the yeast work for several hours until the mixture becomes frothy.

Mix the dry ingredients:

4   pounds whole wheat flour
$1/2$ pound yellow corn meal
$1/2$ pound rolled oats (oatmeal)
1   cup wheat germ
$1/2$ pound whole rye flour
2   cups chopped walnuts or acorns
2   teaspoons salt

Work in $1/2$ pound butter, then pour in liquid ingredients and mix dough. Due to the moisture needs of the cornmeal and oatmeal, the finished dough should be rather moist. Divide dough into 4 or 5 portions and shape into slender loaves, let rise then bake slowly. It will take nearly an hour of slow baking to cook the bread thoroughly. The job can be handled very well in a bake kettle beside the campfire.

Potato Bread

Mix 3 pounds white flour and 2 tablespoons salt with 3 pounds boiled, skinned, mashed, potatoes. Add one can warm beer and knead into dough. Set near heat to ferment and rise. Form the dough into loaves and bake in a hot oven. Warm water and one package of dry yeast may be substituted for the beer if desired.

Hoe Cake

Mix 4 cups corn meal with 1 cup white flour and 2 tablespoons salt. Work in 6 tablespoons bacon grease, add hot water and mix to dough. Mash into small cakes and bake on a flat metal sheet or iron skillet over the fire. The name Hoe Cake was given because the cakes were commonly baked on the polished blades of hoes used by the field hands. Hoe cake isn't fancy. It is a dense, heavy corn cake. Don't expect it to rise like a biscuit. It's good food with a pot of turnips and greens.

Johnny Cake

This sweetened corn cake has been breakfast for many wilderness pilgrims and many generations of their children. It seems to be a recipe that never dies. Mix 4 cups yellow corn meal with 1 cup white flour and 1 teaspoon salt. Work in 6 tablespoons bacon grease and 1 cup ribbon cane molasses then mix to dough with hot water. Form into small cakes. Bake on a flat metal surface over the fire. Because of the sugar content of johnny cakes, they burn easily if the surface is too hot.

Potato Cakes

Boil 3 medium sized potatoes, remove the skins, and mash. Add 2 egg yolks, a splash of wine, 1 teaspoon salt, and 4 tablespoons bacon grease or melted butter. Mix with enough flour to make dough then shape and bake in a hot oven. When done, put a little melted butter over them and dust with brown sugar.

Yam Bread

Boil and mash yams (sweet potatoes and pumpkin will substitute well) to make about 3 cups of pulp. Add 1 package dry yeast, $\frac{1}{2}$ cup raw honey, 2 teaspoons cinnamon, then mix in enough whole wheat flour to make a moist dough. Let the batch rise then knead in 4 teaspoons melted butter and form into small rolls. Bake in a moderate oven. Butter and eat hot.

Pumpkin Shortbread

The frontier woman would do anything to make pumpkin more palatable so her starving brood would eat it. True, she would have preferred to throw all of the gourds out into the snow, but wasting food was considered sinful, and far be it for a Puritan woman to wantonly commit sin!

Mix:

4	cups unbleached flour
4	teaspoons baking powder
$\frac{1}{2}$	teaspoon salt
2	tablespoons ground cinnamon

Then work in $\frac{3}{4}$ cup bacon grease. To this add:

1	cup raw honey
3	cups boiled and mashed pumpkin
1	cup milk

Make into dough and form into biscuit size rolls. Bake in a hot oven. Serve hot with butter.

Berry Pancakes

Gather a double handful of wild berries early in the morning then put together a camp breakfast unequaled anywhere.

Mix:

2	cups whole wheat flour
2	cups unbleached white flour
1	cup corn meal
6	teaspoons baking powder
$\frac{1}{2}$	teaspoon salt

Stir in:

1	cup water (milk if preferred)

$^{1}/_{2}$ cup raw honey
2   eggs
$^{1}/_{4}$ cup bacon grease

Gently fold in the fresh berries. Spoon out onto a hot griddle or skillet and bake on one side until the upper side is full of holes, turn and bake until lightly browned. Be careful, the sugar content of these pancakes makes them burn easily if the griddle is too hot or they are on too long. Serve hot with, or without, butter and syrup.

Corn Tortillas

Now that corn flour is available in the supermarkets (masa harina), it is both convenient and practical to make this tasty, thin corn bread. Mix the corn flour with just enough warm water to make a dough. Roll into balls, $1^{1}/_{2}$ inch in diameter, then roll out or pat into thin sheets about $^{1}/_{8}$ inch thick and 5 inches in diameter. Cook on a hot metal plate over high heat. A griddle or an old steel drum lid works fine. Serve hot with butter. These are quick and easy to make up and work well for feeding hungry kids a quick breakfast.

A little hint for baking tortillas: put the tortilla on the cooking surface and sear one side quickly; then, turn it over and continue cooking until it puffs up into almost a ball with steam. Remove from the heat immediately.

Flour Tortillas

Mix is similar to biscuits. However, only $^{1}/_{3}$ the baking powder and $^{1}/_{2}$ the grease are used and water is substituted for milk.

Mix:

2   cups white flour
$^{2}/_{3}$ teaspoon baking powder
$^{1}/_{2}$ teaspoon salt

Work in $1^{1}/_{2}$ tablespoons grease or cooking oil into dough with enough warm water to make it elastic. Roll into balls, $1^{1}/_{2}$ inch in diameter, then roll ball out into thin sheets about $^{1}/_{8}$ inch thick and 5 or 6 inches across. Bake on a hot metal plate over a hot fire. Serve hot with butter.

Corn Bread in a Skillet

Skillet corn bread is the most practical bread in camp. Besides nutrition, it is so much quicker and easier to make than any other bread.

Mix:

1	cup yellow corn meal
1/2	cup white flour
2	teaspoons baking powder
2	tablespoons sugar

Stir in:

1	egg
2/3	cup milk or water
4	tablespoons grease

Put about 2 tablespoons grease into a cast iron skillet and place on the fire to heat. When the grease in the skillet is smoking hot, pour in the cornbread mix and set back on the fire. Cook until sides and bottom are browned and the top is almost dry, then prop near the fire to finish browning by radiated heat. From start to finish, this takes only about 20 minutes.

Vegetables

We are irritated by the annual weed crop that seems to flourish in our lawns and gardens every spring. The family carving a home out of the wilderness viewed the weed crop as manna from heaven. There were collard greens, pokesalad, dandelions, careless weeds, and a multitude of others. The new crop of greens meant there would be a new variety added to the supper table. Garden crops always included turnips, beets, and other dual use plants, that could be harvested for their greens as well as their roots. The people knew nothing about vitamins or minerals, nutrition or calories, but they knew they had a craving for the fresh greens which became abundant with the coming of spring.

Field and garden crops were carefully planned to produce fresh foods as long as the growing season continued. An example of this would be the planting of corn. One row of corn would be planted in the garden every four days. When the corn matured, all of the ears on the stalks planted at the same time would be ready at the same time. The family would eat off this row until the next row matured, and so on. The field crop pattern was established to produce as many different full crops as possible through the growing season.

The mountain man and his plains counterpart ate from the vegetables and fruits provided by nature. They learned to identify and prepare wild greens, roots, and fruits. Dried fruits, seeds, and nuts went into pemmican to be stored to meet the coming winter.

Greens

The vitamin and iron-rich leaves of many herbaceous plants make up into fine fare for the table. Spinach, mustard, collard, pokesalad, dandelion, beet, turnip, careless weed, and many more greens are edible and delicious, when properly prepared. Preparation follows the same general pattern for any of the leaves listed.

Select small to medium sized leaves and tender stems, gather a pound to a pound and a half of greens for each person to be fed. Pick over the leaves carefully to remove insects and blighted portions. Wash the leaves several times in clear water to remove dirt and sand. While carrying out the cleaning process, have a pot of water on the fire to boil. Chop the tender stems into small pieces and tear the leaves into manageable sizes and pack them tightly into a pot. Pour boiling water over them, add a couple of teaspoons of salt and put on the fire to continue boiling. Let the pot boil for ten minutes, then remove from the fire and pour off the water. The strong, bitter, and hot taste of the greens is removed with the water of the first boil. The greens have now cooked down to only about one fifth of the original volume. Add enough water to cover the greens, put in several chunks of bacon, ham, or salt pork, and salt and pepper to taste. Boil the greens until tender.

The same process is followed for cooking turnips or other strong or bitter root vegetables with greens. Boil the pot of food once, then drain and boil again. Eating the greens is a delight when there is a big pan of hot cornbread to go along with them. Don't quit when the greens and side meat are gone. Go after the "pot-likker", the liquid that the greens were cooked in, with a chunk of cornbread. Cornbread and pot-licker are hard to beat.

Beans

There have been several quasi-historical novels portraying the facts of how the west was won... the truth is that it was won with beans. Every pilgrim that ever outfitted for the wilderness carried a ration of beans. No food has been found that packages so small and goes so far as the lowly bean. Beans also served other purposes besides food.

Several years ago, I was looking into the feasibility of reopening the old Blackhawk Silver Mine located near Winston, New Mexico. From the preserved records, I found that much of the original development work, done in the early 1850s, was done with beans. This was during a period when time and labor were cheap but blasting powder was expensive. Holes were bored with a drill and doublejack, spacing them closer than normal blast holes. The drill holes were filled about one third full of beans then filled with water. After a period of soaking, the holes were stemmed with sand and the beans were left to germinate. Within a week or so, tiny cracks began to develop in the rock. The miners finished breaking the rock with hammer and picks. The waiting time was spent laboriously drilling more holes and loading them with beans. I can only imagine the stench that must have been in the shaft and drift from the soured beans.

Everybody has his favorite recipes for preparing beans. There are so many types of beans that there is no way of covering them without giving them a volume of their own. Some people like beans in thin soup; some like highly spiced beans; some like sweetened beans; and some like to use beans as a matrix for meat, onions, garlic, tomatoes, etc., etc. It is this kind of versatility that makes beans such a useful food.

Preparing beans for cooking is a simple process. The beans are picked through to remove the rocks, chunks of dirt, withered and deformed beans, bugs, and anything else you don't want in the pot. Next, they are washed to remove dirt and dust. Finally, they are put into a pot and soaked for several hours; overnight is generally the best so that they can be put on to cook sometime during the following day. Beans will triple in volume during the soaking and cooking period, so be careful with the quantity selected for cooking and the pot size for soaking. One pound of pinto beans will feed a family of six with enough left over for breakfast.

The camper cooking beans for the first time in the high country of the Rockies is in for a surprise. He will find that, even if the beans have been soaked for 12 hours or more, they will not cook tender. It is almost like trying to cook lead rifle balls. If the camping trip is going to include the mountains, take along a five quart pressure cooker for cooking beans. Beans cooked at, or a few hundred feet above, sea level can be cooked in about 4 hours. Without presoaking, they will cook in only about 240 minutes.

Ham and Beans, Bacon and Beans, Sowbelly and Beans

Cured pork always adds to the flavor of a pot of beans. Use presoaked beans; pinto beans, navy beans, lima beans, butter beans, or any other of the dried beans; with ham, bacon, or salt pork. Put the meat and beans on to cook over a slow fire for about 4 hours, until tender. A thin, clear bean soup results from little or no stirring during the cooking period. Thicker soup can be had by frequent stirring during the last hour of cooking, while really thick soup requires mashing some of the beans. Build them to your liking. (Add salt, pepper, etc. during the last hour.)

Frijoles Nacionales (National Beans)

These are pinto beans as cooked in Mexico. Use a pound of pinto beans, presoak if the altitude increases cooking time. Put in the following:

1	bell pepper (thinly sliced)
2	medium onions (finely chopped)
4	garlic cloves (minced)
6	ripe tomatoes (peel and cut up) or 1 #303 can whole tomatoes
	salt and pepper to taste

Cook slowly over low heat for about 4 hours, stirring only enough to blend the contents but try for a rather clear soup. This is served as a side dish or as an entree in and of itself. It is not overly spiced or hot and is agreeable to most everyone.

Texican Beans

These beans are a meal in themselves. They are spicy and can be made as hot as the eaters would like them. Start with one pound pinto beans, presoaked if necessary. Put the beans on to cook over low heat, using enough water to cover them to a depth of 2½ inches. Let them cook by themselves for about 2 hours. While they are cooking, and in a separate pot, brown 2 pounds coarsely ground or chopped lean beef and add the following to the meat:

3   onions (large, chopped)
2   bell peppers (chopped)
6   cloves garlic (minced)
2   green jalapeno peppers (raw, minced)
8   ripe tomatoes (skinned and cut up) or 1 large can whole tomatoes with juice

Cook all of the above together until done, then add and stir in:

4   ounces chili powder (pure)
2   teaspoons ground cumin
1   teaspoon black pepper

After the beans have cooked for 2 hours, add and stir in the meat mixture. Salt to taste and finish cooking. It is at this point that red pepper can be added to raise the heat to suit the crowd. Stir the beans frequently during the last hour of cooking to prevent sticking and scorching, as well as to thicken the soup. Remember that red pepper is a lot easier to add than it is to take out. Add what you dare, then put the red pepper on the table for those wanting real hot beans.

Fried Beans

This is the way to use leftover beans. Mash the beans to a thick, stiff paste and put into a large cast iron skillet over the fire. Put in about 4 tablespoons bacon grease or cooking oil and mix with the mashed beans. Stir the beans as they cook. Using a spatula as a scraper, scrape the beans from the skillet. When the cooking beans are boiling hot clear through, stir in 1 teaspoon baking powder to make them light and fluffy. Continue until they are almost dry, then form into a loaf and lift out onto a plate. Put several strips of cheese on to melt over the loaf and serve. Fried beans are excellent with almost any meal. A generous helping covered with two eggs, fried sunny-side-up, make a horse of a breakfast!

Green Beans

Planning and tending a garden may seem like a lot of work, and it is. But, having fresh, crisp vegetables either on the table or cooking in the pot is more than a just reward. A kettle of garden fresh green beans makes a repast fit for nobility.

To prepare, thoroughly wash 4 pounds of green beans. Snap them into short lengths and put them into a large kettle. Peel and wash 12 new potatoes, and quarter them into the beans. Chop and add 1 sweet onion. Add enough water to cover them. Salt and pepper to taste and add about an 8 ounce chunk of bacon. Cover and cook slowly over low heat until the green beans are tender and well done. With a pot of vittles like this, who needs anything more?

Sweet Bean Dessert

Mash 3 cups boiled beans and stir in 1 cup brown sugar, 1 teaspoon ground cinnamon, and $1/2$ teaspoon salt. Cook together in a shallow pan over low heat until the mixture reaches the texture of a pudding. Remove from the heat then stir in 1 teaspoon vanilla extract and 3 tablespoons butter. Serve in small quantities.

Corn

Protein is a combination of amino acids, and some of those amino acids are in corn. Another group of amino acids are present in beans. When eaten at the same meal, beans and corn combine to form a complete protein. This combination may not taste like sirloin steak, but the nutrition is the same. It is little wonder that the people of North America have fared so well on combinations such as cornbread with beans or beans with corn tortillas. Though they were ignorant of this fact, the human body seemed to know.

The two foods complement each other in taste as well as nutrition, and stimulates a craving for them.

Farms and gardens of the frontier probably produced more corn than all the rest of the crops put together. Corn was eaten green, dried and parched, ground into meal, pulverized into flour, made into syrup, sugar, starch, and used in combinations of every conceivable nature. Farm animals were fed and fattened on corn. Sour mash was turned into whisky. Corn was in such demand that the farmer had no trouble getting his corn milled to his specifications on the halves, and many times could even strike a better deal.

Steamed Green Corn

This cooking method works well when feeding a large number of people. It can be scaled down, but it works so well that it should be presented full scale. Put 1 inch of water in the bottom of a number 3 wash tub. Stand the tub full of field picked ears; shucks, silks, and all; with the stalk end down. The wash tub should hold about 6 dozen ears when tightly packed. Cover the tub with canvas and put a thick covering of feed sacks over the canvas. Set the tub on a bed of glowing coals and in about 5 minutes heavy steam should be coming from the cover. Let it steam for about 3 minutes then remove. Leave the cover on until ready to serve. Have plenty of butter, salt, and pepper ready and waiting.

Baked Green Corn

Cut the kernels from 8 ears of fresh green corn into a buttered pan. Mix 1 cup milk, 2 eggs, 3 tablespoons white flour, $1/2$ teaspoon salt, and black pepper to your liking, then stir the mixture into the corn. Put 4 tablespoons butter on top and bake at a moderate heat until the liquid has thickened and the top is lightly browned.

Corn Meal Mush

Regardless if today's massive selection of presweetened breakfast cereals talk to you or just lie there and get soggy, corn meal mush is a welcome treat.

Put 3 cups water with a dash of salt on the fire to boil. When it reaches a rolling boil, stir in $2/3$ cup yellow corn meal and cook until thickened. Serve hot. Some like it with butter and honey, others like milk or cream and sugar. Fix it to suit your taste.

Fried Corn Meal Mush

Prepare mush as for eating hot but let it get cold and set several hours. Slice the congealed mush 1/2 inch thick and fry until browned. Serve with eggs and bacon, ham, or sausage, or with honey or syrup.

Green Corn Syrup

Shuck and clean 6 ears fresh green corn. Break the cobs into small pieces, place them in a pot, and add enough water to barely cover the corn. Boil until the volume of water has been reduced by half. Strain liquid into another pot then stir in 1 pound brown sugar and boil until the syrup consistency is right. Check by dipping a spoon into the syrup and lifting it clear of the surface of the liquid. The syrup will drip from the spoon in a characteristic manner. Small, single drops forming rapidly and falling freely indicate the syrup still needs cooking down. Large drops forming and holding until a second drop begins to form then both combining and falling together indicates the syrup is right. When the drop trails a long thin string of syrup, it has passed into the first candy stage.

Parched Corn

Place dry feed corn into a cast iron skillet over a hot fire. Dry cook in this manner until grains are parched brown. They will swell somewhat but will seldom more than double their uncooked size. When done, they may be eaten like nut kernels. This makes an excellent trail food that can be eaten whenever you are hungry.

Another method is to use grease in the skillet in the same way as would be done for popping corn. When done, the kernels are removed from the skillet onto absorbent material to remove the grease, then salted.

Pumpkin

Pumpkin is a squash and may be prepared as such when green or ripe. In the early days of our country, the frontiersman-farmer planted and raised crops to meet both the immediate and long term needs of his household. Pumpkin was one of the vegetables which had a reasonable storage life. However, pumpkin has become synonymous with sweets and spices as a Thanksgiving and Christmas only food. Many of its possibilities have long been ignored and forgotten. Perhaps this is just as well. The best thing that ever happened to a ripe pumpkin was Halloween.

Buttered Green Pumpkin

Green pumpkin is firm and hard. It makes a pot of boiled and buttered squash that is neither mush nor all water. Peel a green pumpkin and remove the pithy seed portion then cut the firm shell portion into bite sized pieces. Place into a pot and put in enough water to just cover the pieces. Add about 1 teaspoon salt and boil until tender then drain and butter. Salt and pepper to taste and serve with any meat dish.

Garden Dinner

For those that don't like squash, or think they don't, this is one to be tried. Any firm, green squash can be substituted for green pumpkin. Pumpkin is preferred for its firmness so that it does not lose its identity with cooking. Other green squashes must not be overcooked and should be added near the end of the cooking period. Leave the peeling on pumpkin or squash if it is tender, it adds color to the dish as well as nutrition.

Brown 2 pounds fresh lean pork in the cook pot, then cook in the following:

1	medium onion
4	peeled ripe tomatoes
2	pounds green pumpkin
2	cups fresh corn (cut from the cob)
1	pound green beans
2	bay leaves

Season with salt and black pepper. Simmer over low heat until vegetables are tender.

Calavasita (Little Pumpkin)

If you have a taste for some genuine Mexico Mexican cooking, this is for you. Being a Texican myself, this is one of my favorites. It is spicy, but does not have to be hot. It is usually prepared mild so that all members of the family, from infant to grandmother, can eat and enjoy it. To liven it up for those who prefer it pepper hot, pepper can be put on at the table.

2-3 pounds meat (fresh pork, chicken, beef, young goat; one or all are used)
2 large onions (chopped)
1 large bell pepper (chopped)
4 cloves garlic (minced)
2-3 pounds green pumpkin (cut to bite size)
4-6 ears fresh green corn (cut from the cob)
6 large ripe tomatoes (peeled and cut)
4 tablespoons pure chili powder
1 teaspoon ground cumin
salt and black pepper to taste

Brown the meat and saute onions, garlic, and bell pepper. Peel and cut up tomatoes and add to meat mixture to provide moisture and cool the sauteed vegetables to prevent burning. Add the rest of the listed vegetables and cover with a tight fitting lid, cook slowly over a low heat to simmer in its own juices. Put in chili powder, cumin, salt, and pepper after the food has cooked tender; cover and simmer for another ten minutes, then serve. Corn or flour tortillas are all that is needed to really make calavasita a feast of the gods.

Baked Pumpkin

Most modern cookbooks treat pumpkin as if it were a sweet, succulent fruit. In truth, the gourd is really quite plain and versatile. There is a high sugar content in the starchy pulp of the ripe pumpkin, about the same as the sweet potato, plantain, and yam. Since these vegetables have similar physical characteristics when cooked, they may be freely substituted for one another in various recipes. The ripe pumpkin can be baked, boiled, fried, stewed, candied, and eaten raw. This way, if you find yourself stuck with a wagon load of pumpkins, you can have something besides pies.

Slices of pumpkin can be baked, laid skin down on a flat baking sheet, as if it were acorn squash. Salt and pepper to taste and cover with butter. Put into bake kettle or oven and bake with moderate heat until tender. If a sweet or candied bake is desired, use brown sugar in place of salt and pepper and sprinkle with cinnamon. This is almost like pumpkin pie without the crust.

Boiled Pumpkin and Stewed Pumpkin

Boiled pumpkin is an over-the-fire variation of sweet baked pumpkin. The seeds and strings are removed and peeling is cut away, then the pulp is cut into chunks and put into a pot with enough water to cover the pieces. This is put on to boil until tender, then drained. A liberal quantity of butter is put in, along with honey or molasses then stirred while sprinkling cinnamon to taste. Serve hot with roast pork or fowl.

Stewing requires pumpkin, sweetener, and spice to be put in with one pint of milk. This mixture is cooked over a low heat until pieces are tender. Put in butter after cooking and serve hot. Overcooking will result in a watery mush.

Pumpkin Boiled in the Shell

This is a real oldie, as old as America itself. Select a pot large enough to hold a whole pumpkin. Cut a hole in the top of the pumpkin, remove the seeds and strings, then cut a thumb-sized hole in the bottom. Put the pumpkin into the pot with boiling water, the hole in the bottom will allow the shell to sink readily. Boil over high heat until the pulp is tender but the outer shell is still hard. Carefully lift the pumpkin from the water and drain then serve hot.

Place the whole pumpkin in the center of the dining table. Give every member of the family a tablespoon and gather them around to their places. After the blessing, all dig in and scoop out a serving and put it on the table in front of them and eat. No fancy linen tablecloth, no plates, just an authentic colonial dinner a la 1700. See, times were hard then, too. Don't forget to put the plate of salt near the head of the table.

Pumpkin Seeds

Eating pumpkin seeds was serious business in the colonies. Food was food, with very few frills. The seeds were saved from the ripe pumpkin and dried on a shallow pan. After collecting the seeds from several pumpkins they were put into the bake kettle and roasted until brown. Eating the seeds differed little from eating sunflower seeds. The little roasted kernels are delightful.

Meat

Before the advent of refrigeration, preservation of meat was limited to drying, salting, sugaring, smoking, pickling, and potting. Fresh meat would last a relatively short time hanging in the meat shed, depending on the climate. Killing time for meat animals usually corresponded with late fall, when the days were cool and nights were cold. Cooler temperatures relieved much of the work pressure of having to race against spoilage. Not too many years ago, fresh meat could be hung in the shade and have a protective crust form over the carcass within a matter of minutes. The crust made the meat almost impervious to insects and helped preserve it during processing. This crust no longer forms on meat hanging in the open air. It has been suggested that the bacteria count in our atmosphere is so high that putrefaction begins almost immediately. Those who remember the old open air butcher shops of the 1930s will recall the crusting effect on the hanging meat.

Most average, twentieth century outdoorsmen, if invited to share a meal with an Indian hunting party or a mountain man of the eighteenth century, would probably be hesitant to eat, or be completely repelled by the food served. The wisest thing to do under those circumstances would have been to eat and enjoy the meal and wait a couple of hours before asking, "What was it?" The people of the prairie, woodlands, and mountains ate far differently than the average family eats today. The game of life was to eat or starve. Any food that would not eat them first was fair game, and if they got first bite it was theirs anyway. Dry land snails, crickets, grass-

149

hoppers, locusts, earthworms, lizards, snakes, and tortoises were all on the menu at one time or another. The white man trapped beaver for their pelts, the Indian ate the carcasses as well. Few sources of protein were overlooked in the wilderness. Normal foods of the early Americans are repugnant to the "civilized" person only because they don't have to subsist on such a bill-of-fare.

Actually, there is nothing wrong with eating grubs and snails, or anything else that has been mentioned. The "wrong" is in the mind; it is a reflex conditioning developed over the formative years. Parents teach their children to eat only certain things. They provide "good" things to eat, and teach that all else is "bad" and should not be put into the mouth. Such training is hard to break, and certainly interferes with trying something new. However, the saying "try it, you'll like it" isn't always true either. Some things just do not tickle the palate. But in a pinch, oh well...it's food!

Colonial Americans raised pigs, chickens, ducks, and geese as industriously as they tended gardens and crops. A few fortunate families owned milk cows but it usually cost them the calf each time they had the cow bred. The owner of the bull took the calf as payment for stud service after the cow came in fresh and would again give milk. He raised the heifers for breeding and sale as milk cows and cut the bull calves which were to be raised for oxen or sold to the wealthy for beef. Even after the beef cattle population had increased to economic proportions, about 1720, poultry still made up the fresh meat diet of most colonials and it would take many more years before beef was common on the frontier.

The ready availability of fresh meat on the frontier and in the wilderness created a completely different picture of pilgrim diet. Still, the similarity of preserving available and excess meat does not belong to late twentieth century technology alone, but dates back well beyond the establishment of the first colony at Plymouth. Meat preservation was an old art even in ancient Egypt, more than 4,000 years ago. For the period of 1700 to 1850, chemical preservatives were used in the guise of salt, sugar, niter, vinegar, alum, wine, smoke, spices, and herbs. Smoke, resulting from the incomplete combustion of hardwood, adds a long list of chemicals to meat. Some of the chemicals, although excellent preservatives, are considered to be unfit for human consumption by today's health standards.

Dried Meat

Jerky, charqui, or whatever you wish to call it, is best made from heavy, dense meats. Beef, buffalo, deer, elk, caribou, moose, and antelope are all excellent for jerking. Basically, the process requires only lean meat, salt and pepper, and some means to dry the meat. There are two basic ways to prepare the meat, one is to cut the meat into thin strips about $1/2$ inch thick, the other is to strip out the muscles so that each piece of meat is surrounded by the muscle sheath (fascia). The muscle stripping method produces the more flavorful jerky but requires more drying time. Most of the time it is better to combine the two methods and strip the smaller muscles and cut the larger ones into strips, a compromise measure to expedite drying.

Roll the meat in a 1 to 1 mixture of salt and black pepper and hang the meat over a drying line set up on a screened-in porch or in a room with good ventilation. The heavy black pepper coating helps keep the flies off of the meat if any get through the screens. Meat dried in this manner will take 2 to 3 weeks to finish out, depending on climate and weather conditions, but it will be well worth the wait. The drying process can be hurried by using the oven of the kitchen stove.

The kitchen oven method dries the meat rapidly and requires neither salt nor pepper. This is excellent for those of you who are on a salt-free diet or don't like pepper. Place the meat on the oven rack so that the pieces do not touch one another, then place the rack in the oven at its highest position. Lower the other rack to its lowest position and put a shallow baking sheet or aluminum foil in position to catch any drips which may fall. Turn the oven on to its lowest possible setting, then prop the door open one or two inches with a small block of wood. The purpose of the oven is to dry the meat, not cook it, so the lower the oven heat, the better. Put the meat on to dry after supper and let it dry over night. Oven drying is a long, slow process if you intend to jerk the meat stripped from a whole deer because there is not enough room to dry more than about five pounds of meat at a time.

The third method of making jerky is similar to the oven method but is for those who want the meat lightly smoked. Again, salt and pepper are optional since drying time is greatly reduced. Hang the meat from a rack in a brick or steel drum oven over a cool, smokey hardwood fire. Cover the oven with a lid to hold the smoke for an hour or so, then slip the lid to one side to allow excess heat to escape and dry the meat as the coals burn out. Drying time will be about 6 hours, depending on the fire. It will help control the oven temperature if water soaked hardwood is used to produce the smoke. Again, remember that you are going to dry the meat, not cook it.

Jerky and Eggs (Machicado)

Cut jerky into thin slivers with a sharp knife, cutting across the grain of the meat. Soak the meat slivers in hot water for 10 to 20 minutes then drain. Stir meat and raw eggs together with salt and black pepper. Put this into a pan and cook up into a fine plate of scrambled eggs and jerky. It sure goes well with a bake kettle of biscuits or a pile of flour tortillas.

Jerky and Beans

Cut or break jerky into pieces and add to a pot of pinto beans. By the time the beans are done, the jerky is tender and adds real brawn to the bean pot.

Jerky and Rice

Cut jerky into thin slivers and put it into a pan with 2 cups water and bring to a boil. Add 1 cup brown rice and 1 small onion, diced. Simmer over a low fire until the rice is tender. Salt and pepper to taste and serve. You may want to add garlic, diced carrots, or parsley to the recipe to go along with the onion. Any way you slice it, jerky is fine fare in the camp.

Jerky and Jerky

In the field, on the trail, or in a canoe, jerky is a welcomed snack. A chunk of jerky in the jaw beats a plug of chewing tobacco or dipping snuff. It is a light weight, ready to eat food that is satisfying and nourishing. As to how long jerky will last and still be edible, I don't know. I found a sizeable chunk of jerky in a pocket of a hunting coat that had not been worn for four years. As I remember, the venison had been jerked the season before the last wearing of the coat. That piece of meat was just as flavorful and satisfying as it was when it was removed from the drying line and sacked for keeping. It is good stuff!

Pemmican

Pemmican is like pumpkin pie... no two mixtures are ever alike, even when concocted by the same individual. The American Indians made pemmican as a trail food and also as a preserved ration to help them through long and lean winters. They used what was in supply at the time and in the area. Generally pemmican contained the following groups: meat, cereal, fruit, nuts, fat.

Now, consider the possibilities to the primitive red man. On the prairie, meat and fat was available from buffalo, cereal from a multitude of grasses, but fruit and nuts may have posed a problem. Likely as not, the meat and cereal served to make that particular batch of pemmican. The next time the same group of people made up a batch, they may have been near a river bottom woodland where all of the groups were available.

It is easy for us to come up with the majority of the needed ingredients with one trip to the local health food store. Since it is so easy, we might as well put together a batch made up of things we like. If you want to do it like the genuine mountain man then you will have to find all of the goodies for yourself. I dare say, my pemmican won't taste like yours, but they will both be high in nutrition if we use ingredients from all of the groups.

Meat

Jerky beef is the most logical choice for making pemmican because it has the best storage life. Freeze dried beef is also a good choice. The meat should be ground or pounded into a coarse flake form. About 1/2 pound of meat (dry weight) should be prepared.

Fat

The best fat available for the mix must be rendered from heavy beef fat. Beef fat is more easily digested than lard and is a harder, or higher temperature, fat than shortening. It does not go rancid as easily as lard, either. Buy about 3 pounds of heavy beef fat from the local butcher. Chop and place it in a pan and bake in the oven at about 350°F until the fat is withered and well browned. There should be about 2 pounds of fat in the pan when the rendering is done. you will not need this much grease but the leftover portion can go to the kitchen grease bucket.

Cereal

Corn, sorghum, millet, oats, wheat, rye, and barley are all good grains. These should be crushed, rolled, or coarse ground so that there is still body to the grain. I recommend a mixture of three or more from the list. It will take $1\frac{1}{2}$ pounds of cereal for the mixture.

Nuts

There are a variety of nuts to choose from. Raw nuts are the best, such as: pecans, walnuts, acorns, and pinon nuts. Use about 2 pounds chopped coarsely.

Fruit

Select whatever dried fruit that strikes the fancy of your palate; raisins, currants, apricots, peaches, apples, and prunes are all good. It will take 1 pound to finish the list for a batch of pemmican. Chop the fruit into a size approaching that of currants or raisins.

Mix all of the dry ingredients with 1 cup of raw honey. After the mixing is completed add hot beef fat in sufficient volume to make a dry, thick dough. Test the dough by taking a handful and squeezing it to see if it will stick together. If it molds and does not fall apart, it is just right. Avoid getting the mix too wet with grease.

The pemmican is now ready to be molded into convenient sized blocks and packaged for the field. Select a suitable mold and line it with waxed paper. Wax paper is easily disposable in a camp fire and also makes a convenient fire starter. Pack the warm pemmican tightly into the mold and fold the paper to seal the package. Remove the packet from the mold and set aside to finish cooling. As the pemmican cools, the grease congeals, making the block nearly as solid as a chocolate candy bar and just about as susceptible to the heat, although it will not be any more liquid than it was when it was mixed. Store the pemmican in the deep freeze, this will insure freshness when you are ready to put it to use. This recipe makes nearly 9 pounds of goodies, enough to get you through breakfast.

Pemmican can be eaten like a candy bar or it may be cooked in water to make a porridge that is not only very tasty but hot as well. A hot bowl of porridge sure is good to start a cold November morning.

Dried Fish

The Indians of the lakes and rivers took fish in great numbers and dried them to tide them over the winter. Small fish were dried whole, while large fish were split down the back and the backbone removed. The method of drying was so simple that it could be done at a fishing camp so that large quantities of fish could be brought back to the main camp already dried and bundled, without having to carry several hundred pounds of water. The drying racks consisted of four to six stakes driven into the ground to support a grillwork made of evenly spaced green sticks of peeled willow or other suitable wood. The racks were tied together with rawhide and stood two to three feet off the ground. The fresh fish were placed on the rack and hot coals were spread on the ground beneath the fish. Heat from the coals rapidly dried the fish while the smoke from damp hardwood added in curing the meat as well as keeping the insects away. The same drying method will work on other meats cut in thin strips.

Trout and salmon are excellent when cured in this manner. Alaskan Indians call dried salmon "squaw candy" and it is enjoyed by all that have occasion to try it. Many combination dishes can be prepared with dried fish. Combinations including rice are perhaps the most common, but noodles, macaroni, and potatoes make good eating too. I like dried salmon chipped up in scrambled eggs with hash brown potatoes to start the day in the hunting camp. Two or three slabs of salmon in the day pack helps when the hungries attack during the afternoon.

Salmon and Rice

$1/2$ pound brown rice
4   ounces dried salmon
1   medium onion
4   ounces sharp cheddar cheese
Use a pot with a tight fitting lid and bring to a boil about one

quart of water. Put in the rice, chips of salmon, and diced onion. Remove the pot from high heat and set to simmer slowly until the rice is done. Shave the cheese into the pot and let it melt using the heat of the cooked rice. Salt and pepper to taste and serve. You may want to color the pot with dried parsley or bell pepper if you happen to have it in your pack. This dish is also good without the cheese.

Salt Meat

Had there been no salt pork, the armies and navies of the world may not have been able to operate outside the boundaries of their home forts and ports. This was the least expensive and surest method of preserving and transporting large quantities of meat, except for driving a live herd along with the troops or billeting a herd in the holds of vessels. Salt pork was brought to America by the first settlers to arrive at Plymouth and, in the ensuing years, salt packed pork fed the colonists through the hard winters.

Preparation of salt pork starts with cutting the meat and fat into large chunks. The pieces of meat can be any size as long as the thickness does not exceed about 2 inches. All bone must be removed from the meat. The meat is then placed into a vat of brine to soak for at least 12 hours. Preparation of the brine is as follows:

Dissolve 3 pounds salt and $1/4$ pound alum in each gallon of water. This will take much stirring and a water temperature of 200°F. The quantity of salt is slightly below that required for super saturation but it is more than sufficient.

After the meat has soaked for at least 12 hours, remove and shake off the excess brine, then roll the meat in dry salt. A white crust should completely cover the meat chunks. Line the inside of a wood or cardboard box with a clean white cloth, then lightly pack the box with meat and rock salt until it is full. Fold the cloth over the top of the meat and store in a cool dark place.

Corning is another form of salting, hence corned beef. Corned beef preparation differs slightly from that of salt pork. Use the basic brine mixture as given for pork but add $1/2$ pound of saltpeter (niter) to the mix. Prepare the beef the same as was done for pork, removing all bone. The beef chunks are placed into the brine and left to soak for two weeks, three for large chunks. The pieces of beef will turn a deep red color during the soaking. After the allotted time, remove the meat and shake off the excess brine, then roll each piece in dry salt and wrap separately in clean white cotton cloths. Tie each bundle securely and hang in a cool, dark, well ventilated place. The corning process can be used on deer, elk, moose, antelope, buffalo, and caribou as well as on beef.

Using salted meat requires washing, soaking, or boiling to remove excess salt, depending on the use the meat is to be put to. Sometimes, merely washing removes enough salt so that the remainder works into flavoring the pot. Other times, boiling the meat for 10 to 15 minutes then frying will make it palatable for eating with eggs and biscuits, etc.

Fried Salt Pork

Slice the desired quantity of salt pork into $\frac{1}{2}$ inch thick pieces. Put the sliced meat into a pan of water and boil for about 5 minutes, remove the pork from the salty water and season to taste with black pepper. Roll the peppered meat in flour and fry in grease until brown. Don't forget to pour out the salty water, it doesn't make good soup.

Boiled Salt Meat

Use either lean salt pork or corned beef. Wash the meat to remove the salt cake then put the meat into a pot with enough water to cover and boil for one hour. Pour off and discard the salty water and replace with fresh water to cover the meat and boil until the meat is tender. Boiled salt meat may be served sliced or it may be chunk cut into a pot of cabbage or greens; either way it is good eating.

Salt Meat in a Stew

Use either lean salt pork or corned beef. Wash the caked salt from the meat and boil in water for $\frac{1}{2}$ hour. Remove the meat and discard the salt water. Cut the meat into chunks and boil until nearly tender, then add cut vegetables and simmer until done. The meat will provide most, if not all, of the salt needed to season the stew. Taste test the stew after it is done before adding more salt... it is easier to add salt than to take it out.

157

Salt Meat for Sausage

Many hunters make sausage from the deer that they got during the hunting season. If you've ever made your own, you know that fresh pork is not the easiest meat to grind. Fresh pork balls up and rolls in the grinder rather than cutting. Salt pork is firm and grinds with ease, even the fat. Wash the salt cake off of the pork chunks and grind it into the venison at a ratio of 3 pounds of salt pork to 7 pounds of venison. The salt content of the meat will be sufficient for the sausage mix.

Potting Meat

A popular and simple method of preserving meat was cooking the meat, then packing it in lard. This type of preservation required salting and spicing of the meat to aid in preservation. Pan sausage was prepared as follows:

5	pounds ground pork
5	pounds ground beef (or venison, elk, etc.)
3	tablespoons salt
$1/2$	ounce black pepper
1	tablespoon (mild) red pepper
4	tablespoons (hot) red pepper
1	ounce ground sage

Mix thoroughly in a large pan and roll into balls about 2 inches in diameter. Mash into thin flat patties and fry until well done.

A large crockery jar was washed, then sterilized by pouring scalding grease from the sausage renderings into the jar. The grease was then poured back into the cooking pot and reheated to frying temperature. Hot sausage patties were then transferred from the cook pot into the crockery jar, carefully laying them so that a small space separated each patty. After 3 or 4 layers were stacked in this manner, scalding grease was then poured to fill the voids between patties. the layering continued, layer after layer until the jar was full to about 2 inches from the top. The last 2 inches was then poured with scalding hot grease and a clean cloth cover was stretched over the top of the jar and tied with a string. The grease congealed to a solid, air-tight, and impervious seal protecting the meat.

Using the meat was a reverse of the packing process. Some of the covering grease was put into a skillet or pot and heated to frying temperature over the fire. The desired number of patties were removed from the top layer of sausage and placed into the cooking vessel. Refrying removed the soaked grease and the meat was ready for the table. The hot grease from the skillet was carefully poured back into the jar, scalding and sterilizing the void space exposed to the air, sealing the contents again.

Beef patties can be prepared and preserved in the same manner, using renderings from heavy carcass fat to provide the sealing. Continued preservation of the meat depends on the care the pot receives. There is a story of a ranch hand who had a pot hanging from the rafters of his line shack. In the old days, the ranch hand worked from dawn to dark then took care of his horse before he took care of himself. This man always ate in the dark. He reached over head and felt out several meat patties then ate them cold with a chunk of bread. He was hungry and didn't need a light to find his mouth. One day he happened to arrive at the cabin before dark and when he looked at his meat patties they appeared to be covered with rice. How long he had been sharing his supper with the maggots, he didn't know, but he did change his ways.

Head Cheese or Souse

A variation of potting is the making of souse. This employs herbs, spices, and pickling and is used to preserve the meat products that ordinarily go to waste in the home processing of meat. Tripe, pig snouts, hearts, tongues, and other parts are all cut and placed together in a pot of water to boil. This meat is cooked until tender and well done. Bone joints, tendons, and skin are boiled in a separate pot to remove and concentrate gelatin. Boiling time for the gelatin pot is about 6 hours. The solids are removed and the liquid is boiled down until the gelatin will hang to the spoon in drops almost twice the size of those of plain water. The cooked meat is then removed from the other pot and allowed to boil for about one hour in the gelatin. During this period, salt, pepper, and ground mustard are added. Remove the mixture from the fire and allow to cool down to a point where the meat can be handled but the gelatin has not begun to congeal. Add apple cider vinegar to the cooled mixture, in a ratio of about $\frac{1}{2}$ pint to the gallon of gelatin and meat. Using a perforated spoon, scoop the meat from the pot into a clean, shallow crockery bowl, packing the meat as tightly as possible. Flow the clear gelatin vinegar liquid from the pot over the meat to form a gelatin cover. Cover the bowl with a clean white cotton cloth and tie cover in place.

The congealed gelatin and vinegar that souse contains provides a preserving layer over the meat, much like the grease did in potting sausage. Storage of souse, as with other preserved meats, requires a cool, dark place. Souse is served by slicing with a sharp knife, then cutting away the covering $\frac{1}{2}$ inch of clear gelatin. It is eaten cold as a jellied meat and makes excellent sandwiches with heavy, whole grain bread. Once a bowl of souse has been cut into, it must be eaten within a few days or it will spoil. It cannot be resealed.

Smoke Cured Meat

The smoke preservation and cooking of meats enjoys a popularity that will falter only after the world's supply of hardwoods is exhausted. Wood smoke provides not only flavor and aroma but preservatives which lend themselves to successful meat storage. The incomplete combustion of hardwood forms tars, distillates, and chemicals which permeate the meat, stopping or retarding the bacterial action responsible for putrefaction. Smoke cured hams of age are as prestigious as old vintage wines.

Preparation of fresh pork for curing as ham requires rubbing the meat down with a mixture of salt, sugar, and saltpeter in equal amounts. As much of the mixture as possible must be rubbed into the meat. A hanging loop made of clean cotton cord is attached to each piece of meat to suspend it in the smoke chamber. A covering of cheesecloth or gauze fabric tightly wrapped and tied around the ham is preferred by some people. The covering provides dust protection to meat that will hang in storage any length of time.

Fresh side meat being prepared for bacon should be lightly rubbed with the sugar, salt, and saltpeter mixture so that sliced bacon will not be too salty when fried and eaten. Attach a clean cotton cord for hanging and wrap with cloth if desired.

A smokehouse is not a complicated structure to build. It may

THE SMOKEHOUSE

The primary function of the smokehouse is to cure meat at a low temperature in a heavy wood smoke environment. The house need not be a fire proof structure as the heat is controlled by a damper on the smoke pipe and the draft on the fire box. Wood or wood and sheet metal construction is satisfactory. The house should have a floor to keep the vermin out and a lock on the door to keep the neighbors out. Drip pans beneath the hanging meat makes clean-up much easier after each use. The ideal location for the smokehouse is on a mound of earth so that the fire box can be located below the level of the floor. This puts the smoke in near the bottom of the house assuring a heavy smoke filled atmosphere.

Some smoke houses are as small as a whisky barrel, the average is about the size of an outhouse. The key to good smoked meats is patience — smoking takes time. Any meat is a candidate for the smokehouse.

© Allen K. Johnston Wichita Falls, Texas   1979

PLATE 46

161

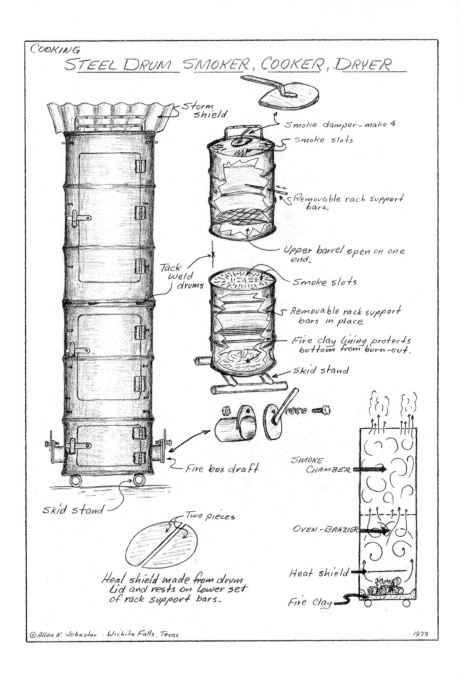

STEEL DRUM SMOKER, COOKER, DRYER

Storm shield

Smoke damper - make 4

Smoke slots

Removable rack support bars.

Upper barrel open on one end.

Smoke slots

Removable rack support bars in place

Fire clay lining protects bottom from burn-out.

Skid stand

Tack weld drums

Fire box draft

Skid stand

Two pieces

Heat shield made from drum lid and rests on lower set of rack support bars.

SMOKE CHAMBER

OVEN - BRAZIER

Heat shield

Fire Clay

© Allen K. Johnston - Wichita Falls, Texas

1979

Plate 47

162

be constructed with a few 2 X 4s for framing and covered with corrugated sheet metal, from two 55 gallon drums, or even a wooden structure. Basically, the smokehouse is only a smoke chamber. It will get warm but not hot. Smoke is drafted into the smoke house by way of a stove pipe connecting the house to a fire box several feet away. The fire box can be a small brick enclosure with a sheet metal lid or a small steel drum. Some sort of damper control is needed to limit the intake of air so that the fire will continue to burn without blazing.

A hot fire is built in the open fire box and allowed to burn down to a bed of coals. Several logs are then placed on the coals and the box closed. Air is drafted through the damper on the box while heat carries the smoke through the stove pipe into the smokehouse. Since the house is always cooler than the fire box, smoke will continue to move into the house. Dampers on the house allow smoke to escape from the house so that free movement of smoke will be guaranteed. Always use hardwood for smoking meats.

Once the smoke is moving into the smokehouse, close the door, set the dampers, and let the smoke do the rest. You will still have to tend the fire, adding wood 3 or 4 times a day, until the meat has been smoked. From 15 to 20 days in the smokehouse will produce fine bacon and about 30 days will cure small to medium hams. Large hams take 45 to 60 days for curing. It was not uncommon for the farm family to leave the meat hanging in the smokehouse for several months, occasionally restarting the smoke fire and smoking the meat more.

Smoking meat for preservation requires cool smoke. Any pork must be cooked before it is safe to eat, even after 60 days in the smokehouse. Remember that pork is the host to the trichina worm and eating raw pork is an invitation to a personal case of trichinosis. Cool smoke will not kill the trichina. Smoke cooking of meats requires hot smoke and the wood or wood framed smokehouse is not suited to this kind of cooking. A smoker made of two drums, as illustrated in Plate 47, is suited for both cool and hot smoking, and is the best medium sized smoker I have found.

Smoke Cooked Meats

Any meat—whether fish or fowl, large animal or small—can be

163

smoke cooked to delight the taste buds. Prepare the meat as you would for baking or broiling. If you like to marinate meat or fish before baking or broiling, then make up your private gastronomic delight and do your thing. When the meat is to your liking, put it into the smoker and smoke it in a hot, heavy-smoke environment for about 6 hours if it is a turkey-sized morsel, 4 hours for chickens, and 10 to 12 hours for something large like a ham. Watch the progress of the smoke and heat, sometimes the heat is higher than anticipated and the meat is done an hour or two sooner than expected. If the heat is lower than desired, it may spoil the dinner party because the meat is still too raw to eat.

There are several smoke cookers on the market today. Some are excellent and others are completely unsuited for smoking. The smoker must close down tight enough to hold the smoke in the upper chamber, but has to have a damper to control the heat and smoke flow. The fire chamber must be far enough from the cooking rack to keep from burning or overcooking the meat. The best cooker shape is similar to a barrel, a tall cylinder. Some of the kettle shaped cookers can be used if a metal baffle is made to separate the fire chamber into two sections so the meat can be placed on one side of the rack, protected and away from the fire. The idea is to use a cooker that provides, in some way or another, plenty of smoke with indirect heat to the meat. Let the hot smoke do the cooking.

Barbecue

Smoke cooked meat differs from barbecue in flavor, texture, and method of cooking. Smoked meat is strong smoke flavored and dry, while barbecue is lighter flavored and juicy. Cooking barbecue requires a more direct heat with less smoke density. The meat is cooked slowly in a smoky, oven-like heat of about 225°F. Properly cooked barbecue beef will have a thin black crust overlying a dark inner band about 1/4 inch thick with the remainder of the meat a well done gray color. It should be very tender and juicy, even if the cut of meat selected is one of the tougher sections of the beef. About 4 to 6 hours should be allotted for cooking barbecue, but be sure to test the meat occasionally with the tines of a fork to prevent overcooking. Each hardwood produces its own unique flavored smoke and imparts it to the meat. Some of the favorite barbecue hardwoods are oak, hickory, and mesquite.

The home barbecue cooker may be a pot shaped cooker with a dome lid. There are several backyard cookers that will fill the bill. Build a hot hardwood fire in the pot and let it burn down to coals, then add more wood to the coals and cover to suffocate the flames. The selected meat should be salted and peppered to taste and placed on the rack in the cooker about 4 inches above the coals. Set the dampers to maintain a heat that will make a drop of water sizzle on the cooker lid. If the drop stays in a ball and rolls off of the lid, the fire is too hot. If the drop wets the lid and leaves a steaming wet streak, the fire is too low. Turn the meat periodically so that it cooks evenly. Do not apply any sauce or baste to the meat wile cooking. Save the sauce to pour over the meat after it is cooked, sliced, and served.

Barbecue Ranch Style

When it comes time to cook for the gun club feed, there is too much meat to do it in the usual home barbecue cooker. The ranch method works well for feeding large numbers of people at a time. The method can be scaled down to cook for a single family. Suppose we need to cook 200 pounds of beef. For this chore we will need to dig a hole behind the range house, the dimensions being about 2 feet deep, 4 feet wide, and 12 feet long. Move as much loose dirt out of the hole as possible, trimming the sides evenly, and piling the dirt well back from the working area. Sprinkle the area with water to settle the dust, then fill the hole with hardwood and set it ablaze. Gasoline, kerosene, and diesel fuel all taste horrible and take a long time to completely burn out of the pit. Just a little of the fuel left in the soil will ruin the barbecue. Crumpled paper targets from last month's shoot saturated with cooking oil are good fire starters for a cooking pit. Continue to add wood until a deep bed of coals has been established, then add one more lay and let it get started. Now comes the part that may sound ridiculous: put the meat right on top of the coals and burning hardwood. Cover the pit immediately with sheet metal. Old metal beer and soft drink signs are ideal for this. Covering will smother the fire and steam from the meat juices cool the pit down. The

165

sheet metal signs cover the pit well enough to retain the heat, but fit loose enough to admit sufficient air to keep the cooking going. Gauge the progress of the cooking by observing the smoke issuing from the pit. As long as there is plenty of smoke curling out from around the pieces of sheet metal, everything is going well. If the smoke dies out, open the top of the pit for a few minutes to give it more air, then re-cover and let the cooking continue. The meat will not stick to the wood or ashes. Tend the pit with a pitchfork and gloves, turning the meat periodically. Cooking time will be 4 to 6 hours. When the meat is done, transfer it to a number three wash tub and cover with a folded bed sheet. When everything is ready, ring the dinner bell.

Prairie Butter

One of the delights passed on to the white man by the Indian was prairie butter. This is made by roasting the long leg bones of deer, elk, buffalo, beef, etc., thoroughly cooking the marrow in the bone cavities. The bones are then removed from the fire and carefully split by beating them with an ax or tomahawk while supporting them on a rock or other hard surface. The marrow is then scooped out and eaten on bread or biscuits as butter. The Indians considered this a delicacy and wasted none of it on bread, but spooned and licked the bones clean.

Calf "Delicacies"

Whether called mountain oysters, calf fries, or any other name, the testicles of calves or goats are a delicacy difficult to equal. It was said that actor John Wayne would interrupt the filming of a multimillion dollar production to travel 600 miles to a branding just to eat lunch.

The calf scrotum is cut open and the testicle is removed and, without any preparation other than salt and pepper, are ready for cooking in shallow hot grease in a skillet. These morsels are seldom available through the supermarket and are generally obtained only through close coordination with a benevolent rancher. If you are so lucky as to obtain a package of them you are in for a delight.

Mussels

Outdoor eating experiences are incomplete without trying fresh water mussels (the clam unio). These are easily located in shallow water around the edges of ponds and lakes. Gather enough for the meal, 5 or 6 apiece, and place them into a bucket of clear, clean water for 12 to 24 hours so they will clean themselves of mud. Fill a pot or bucket with fresh water and add a handful of salt to bring it to a vigorous boil, then drop in the clams. Let the clams boil vigorously for about an hour and a half, drain and serve. The shells will open and removal of the clam is easily accomplished with the end of a knife blade by cutting the adductor muscle from the shells. You may now pop the clam into your mouth and eat. A more tasty morsel from the lake larder is hard to find.

The tastes of your companions may differ to the point that it is necessary to use the clam as an obscure part of the pot. If this is the case, prepare the clams for boiling as stated above, but only parboil them. That is, drop them into boiling water and let them stay long enough to open the shell, then drain off the water and remove the meat from the shell. Chop the clams into small pieces and put them into a chowder, file, or stew and let them cook until tender.

A delicious lacustrine stew contains chopped clams, peeled crawdad tails, boned fish, and chunks of turtle all boiled together with onions, turnips, turnip greens, carrots, garlic, and celery. Spicing this is up to the cook. File powder, cumin, oregano, peppers, etc., are all a matter of taste, but this has to be served over well done brown rice.

Turtles

Here is a critter that is responsible for taking fish from our stringers, muskrats from our traps, and untold ducklings and goslings from their mothers. Turtles are fair game in the outdoors and make a grand feast for a hungry tribe. There are several varieties of turtles available to the hunter and they are all good. The easiest one to work with is the soft-shell turtle; but the old snapper can be cleaned up too. Watch the snapper; he may appear to be dead but don't take chances with his beak. As a kid, I was told that if a turtle

167

got ahold of you that it wouldn't turn loose until it thundered. Another old wives' tale concerning the turtle was that for food, kill the turtle at night in the winter and early in the morning in summer. I have never been able to find out why, so I've always killed them as was convenient and they all turned out about the same, winter or summer.

Kill the turtle and hang it from a tree by the back flippers. Cut off the head and let it bleed well. After body movements have about quit, cut the bottom shell from the top and carefully remove the shell, cutting the skin and connective tissue leaving the legs, neck, and tail attached to the top shell. The care here is to prevent the rupture of the gall bladder which would ruin the meat. Next, remove the liver with the gall bladder and the rest of the entrails. Wash the turtle well, then start removing the meat from the bottom plate. Cut the legs, neck, and tail from the back and remove the skin. Last, cut the meat from the shell... it will take time and patience but it is worth it. Some say there are 100 different kinds of meat on a turtle. I suppose they are partly right, because there is both light and dark with several shades in between.

Now that the meat is off the critter it is time to think about making up the feed. If you want turtle a la carte, then put some bacon drippings into a skillet and put the meat in to fry. Salt and pepper to taste and eat as soon as it is done.

Turtle Soup

Take the meat from a fair sized turtle, one with a 9 or 10 inch shell, and put into a pot with bacon grease and brown. Cut up a large onion, several carrots, and 2 medium potatoes. Salt and pepper, add water and cook until the potatoes are well done. Cut up 2 more medium potatoes and cook until these are done. This allows the first batch of potatoes to cook to pieces and thicken the soup while leaving some potato for identity. From this point on, the individual cook takes over. Add tomatoes or peas, or anything else that your taste dictates to make that just-right pot of soup or stew. By the way, place that shell over an ant bed and let the ants pick out every last piece of meat. The clean shell can be used to make a flask or box. If you don't want it, try taking it to the next club shoot. Somebody will trade you something for it.

Water

Good drinking water has always been a luxury, although the people of this country seldom recognize it as such. Water has always been taken for granted like the warmth of the sun and the air we breathe. Byron said, "'Till taught by pain, man knows not what good water is worth." Since the beginning of civilization, the people have been aware of the dangers of polluted water and even used pollution as a weapon against their enemies. Death and disease, as well as life and health, arise from water. A clear, sparkling stream running swiftly over a clean, rocky channel in the sunshine looks harmless and inviting to the pilgrim. The water is cool and sweet to the taste; certainly it must be good. A long refreshing drink replenishes his strength and he continues on upstream only to find, just around the next bend in the stream, a dead and rotted elk lying half in the water. Or maybe he found nothing to indicate pollution but was warned to keep to his side of the stream by a settler who had sickness and death in his cabin. No, not even the wary Indian or alert woods-wise mountain man had the instinct or ability to judge the potability of water.

There are those who take to the woods for hiking, hunting, fishing, and camping who still think that they are capable of judging the quality of the streams, lakes, and springs that they come across in their journeys. Fortunately, some of us who have done this on many trips have been lucky. There are others that have contracted the amoeba, typhoid fever, diarrhea, or a gut ache and argue that it had to come from the last cafe where they ate. They are sure it couldn't have been the water from the beautiful mountains.

Raw water from any locality needs treatment of some sort to render it safe for drinking. There are so many simple methods of decontaminating water that there is no excuse for using raw water. Here are a few methods.

Boiling Water

Boiling water is a recognized method of decontamination that has been used for hundreds of years. It can be argued that this is not so, but the people of the world have used boiled beverages for drinking for centuries. Tea, coffee, barks, roots, and herbs boiled in water have been prepared for both the sick and healthy through the ages. Boiled water tastes flat and adding flavoring makes up for the taste. Someone, or some group of people, found a relationship between water and disease long ago, but it wasn't until the work done by Pasteur that a "scientific" explanation was offered.

Whiskey and Water

This is a most enjoyable way to purify a glass of water, it also works by the jug or barrel full. For decontamination purposes; about 4 ounces of 180 proof, eight ounces of 90 proof, or ten ounces of 80 proof is added to 5 gallons of clean water. Double if the water is known to be polluted. It is up to the personal taste when mixing by the glass. On shipboard, during the era of exploration and colonization, when the drinking water went bad, rum was mixed with the water to disguise the foul taste; it also, whether the captain knew it or not, kept down sickness.

Sodium Hypochlorite

This comes in several forms: liquid, household chlorine bleach, powdered chlorine disinfectant under several trade names for swimming pools, and as "Halazone" tablets for drinking water purification. If you are using the liquid bleach, put in one teaspoon of bleach for each gallon of water. The powdered disinfectant needs only one teaspoon for each five gallons of water. Halazone tablets usually do the job with one tablet per quart of water. Follow directions on the package label. Let the water stand for half an hour before drinking.

Iodine

About 3 drops of tincture of iodine from the first aid kit for each quart of water will kill the bugs. Give the iodine about 30 minutes to work on the water before drinking. The water will have a slightly bitter taste and smell like disinfectant but it sure beats some of the miseries.

Beverages

Beverages for the table, for quenching thirst in the field, and for leisurely drinking ranged from blackberry tea and barley coffee to whiskey. Fruits and berries were pressed and the juices used to flavor light drinks as well as to make wines and ciders. Herbs, leaves, and barks were used for teas and grains went into coffees, beer, and distilled spirits.

Perhaps the term "tea" should be used in reference to light beverages because the luxury of having real tea to drink was seldom realized. Tea was not seen often in America until the 1750s when the colonies were in better financial position to make the import of such luxury items to America a paying business. Coffee should receive similar treatment, although there is an account of a ration of coffee that was issued to the people of one colony in early 1700. Many of the colonists were unimpressed with the "delicacy" after having boiled the unroasted beans tender and eaten them. By the time the shipment was used up, however, the colonists were avid coffee drinkers.

Teas from Leaves

The preparation of teas begins with the gathering of the leaves. Young and tender leaves are picked and spread out on a tray to be dried in the sun. The leaves are first washed with clear water to remove the dust and insects. After drying, the leaves are packed tightly into jars and capped with a lid. There is no need to shred the leaves like modern tea, unless you want to. Brewing a beverage from the leaves is no different from brewing tea leaves. Some of the useable leaves are as follow: raspberry (hyperion tea), sage, blackberry, goldenrod, grape, four leafed loostrife (liberty tea), sassafras.

Teas from Barks

Strips of bark are peeled from young saplings and small branches. The bark is washed, then laid out on a tray to dry in the sun. The strips are then broken up into small pieces and packed into jars to be used as needed. Brewing teas from bark is the same as leaf tea. A few of the barks are: birch, hickory, walnut, sassafras, persimmon.

Teas from Berries

Ripe berries are collected, washed, and sun dried. In drying berries, care must be taken that they are never laid out more than one berry deep on the tray so that they will dry rapidly rather than spoil. Many times, in winter, dried berries can be found attached to the dead remains of the parent plant. Brewing tea from dried berries is also the same as tea leaves. Suitable berries for berry tea include: raspberry, blackberry, elderberry, sumac, juniper.

Other Teas

A few of the wilderness teas which do not fit the previous categories are those made from rose hips, hickory nuts, and corn stalks. When things get bad enough that corn stalks have to replace everything listed so far, the outlook will be very bleak.

Rose hips are the swollen ovaries of the wild or domestic rose. They are also called rose apples and develop after the petals of the rose have fallen away. Rose hip tea is made by using either green fruit or dried fruit. The rose apples are split and dropped into boiling water and boiled for several minutes, then set aside to cool. The liquid is then poured off and may be used hot or cold. Rose hips are rich in vitamin C and may also be eaten raw to utilize this resource.

Walnuts are used for tea when the nut is green. It is boiled in water until a green color is imparted to the liquid then the nuts are removed. The liquid is sipped as a hot tea.

Coffee from Grains

Cereal grains make good coffees, and may be the answer to the coffee jitters suffered by some people. The general instructions for making grain coffee are simple. Wash the grain to remove dust and chaff, then put it into a pot of boiling water and boil until a few of the grains have split open. Drain the water off of the grain and spread it over the bottom of a large, shallow tray to dry. Put the dry grain into the oven and roast until parched. When done, the grain will be dark brown or almost black. The grains can be ground or used as they come from the oven. Brew the beverage as you would modern coffee. Interesting flavors are developed when grain coffees are mixed with pure ground coffee.

Barley probably makes the best grain coffee when it is used by itself, but rye and grain sorghum are also hard to beat. Roasted and parched acorns, walnuts, crushed walnut shells, pumpkin shells, and corn cobs have been used as coffee. Sometimes life on the frontier was mighty rough.

Juices and Other Uses of Fruits and Berries

As fruits and berries ripened in the woods and meadows, the people took down their fruit presses and made all of the juices that time and season allowed. Berry and fruit flavored drinks were a delightful addition to the table after a winter of teas from leaves, barks, and grains. It was a new season, and to celebrate it with taste-awakening fresh juices was most enjoyable. Some of the juices went into jellies, marmalade, conserves, and many other types of sweet fruit preserves. Wines and ciders worked in the darkness of the root cellars, while sweet cider was available to all takers. The juice of the peach and pear went into both sweet and hard peachy and peary. The work was long and hard, but this was the only way to prepare for another year, to take what was given and put back all that could be saved for leaner times and use and enjoy the bounty, wasting as little as possible. These were times when there was no other way and, really, nothing else to do.

Everything was used. A jug of sweet cider that had sat too long received a small scrape of yeast, which set to work making hard cider. If the hard cider worked too long it passed beyond being palatable and became vinegar. Into the vinegar went vegetables or meat to be pickled. There was seldom waste.

Strong Beverages

Beer was made in the colonies, in the roadhouses, in the home, on the farm, and everywhere except the church or meeting house. Some of the beer was good and some was close to poison, but everybody brewed beer. Most of the old recipe books treat the brewing of beer as being a process as common as churning butter, passing along a list of common ingredients without reference to quantities. There was little thought that in a short span of 250 years that there would be millions of people in America who never saw a cow being milked, butter being churned, or beer brewing in the home keg.

The beer brewing process started with the malting of barley. Grain barley was steeped in water until it germinated, then, just before it went to sprout, it was put into the brewing vat with water, sugar, and yeast. The modern mountain man can buy malt in the supermarket in two and five pound cans, sugar in bags, and yeast in packets. Good beer is also available in cans, bottles, and kegs already cold and ready to drink. In "Ye Old Roadhouse" a cold beer was a mug dawn from a keg that was standing in the shade.

A word of warning in making home brew, it can be poisonous if it is allowed to go too far before it is bottled. The trick in brewing is to catch it just before it starts to go to vinegar, pouring off a sweet bubbling brew. If it comes off too late you will find that even a little acetic acid in the beer will do strange things to the stomach and bowels.

Other brews were made for leisurely drinking. Metheglin was brewed from the beans of the honey locust, sugar, water, and yeast. Beware of the use of the black locust bean, it is poisonous. It has a toxalbumin similar to the castor bean. Metheglin and mead are old Druid drinks dating to antiquity. Both of these drinks made it to America with the first settlers and were used for many years in the colonies. The honey locust was cultivated in Virginia to supply the large demand for the beans. Mead, however, required only honey, water, and yeast to brew.

Distilled Spirits

Rum was New England's great contribution to the slave trade. A corner of the triangle structure of the slavery market was the New England rum making industry. Slaves were bought on the shores of Africa and paid for with rum, then they were taken to the West Indies where they were sold to plantation owners and paid for with molasses. The molasses was shipped to New England where it was sold and turned into rum by the distilleries. The plantation owners of the South may still carry the vocal blame for the slave trade, but it could not have happened the way it did were it not for the good people of New England who realized a fine profit from the action.

Throughout the populated area of early America, distilleries turned out whiskeys made from the grain that was grown locally. Corn, rye, and barley went into the mash vats to ferment, each grain making its own characteristic whiskey. Both the domestic and export markets for whiskey were strong, making corn, rye, and barley good cash crops when other markets were weak.

Chili

No cookbook from the Southwest would be complete without the mention of chili—well there, it's been mentioned, so the section is complete.
ENJOY!

Classic Adventures

Great Western Train Robberies transports you to the scenes of many of the West's most celebrated adventures. Each authentic episode details the robbery, follows the lawmen through the tracking and investigation, summarizes the notable incidents surrounding the crime, and reports the final outcome. Much of the material, including the many photographs, has never before been released from the railroad files.

Great Western Train Robberies
Don DeNevi
5 1/2 x 8 1/2, SC, 202 pp.
ISBN 0-88839-287-7
12.95

Spring 1995

The Lonesome Lake Trilogy

A trilogy of stories by the Edwards family about their fascinating life in the Bella Coola area.

Ruffles on my Longjohns
Isabel Edwards
5 1/2 x 8 1/2, SC, 297 pp.
ISBN 0-88839-102-1 17.95

Ralph Edwards of Lonesome Lake
Ed Gould
5 1/2 x 8 1/2, SC, 296 pp.
ISBN 0-88839-100-5 12.95

Fogswamp
Living with Swans in the Wilderness
Trudy Turner and Ruth M. McVeigh
5 1/2 x 8 1/2, SC, 255 pp.
ISBN 0-88839-104-8 11.95

Bootlegger's Lady
Ed Sager, Mike Frye
5 1/2 x 8 1/2, SC, 286 pp.
ISBN 0-88839-976-6 9.95

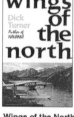

Wings of the North
Dick Turner
5 1/2 x 8 1/2, SC, 288 pp.
ISBN 0-88839-060-2 14.95

Yukon Lady
Hugh Maclean
5 1/2 x 8 1/2, SC, 192 pp.
ISBN 0-88839-186-2 11.95

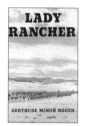

Lady Rancher
Gertrude Minor Roger
5 1/2 x 8 1/2, SC, 184 pp.
ISBN 0-88839-099-8 12.95

Pioneering Aviation in the West
As told by the pioneers
Lloyd M. Bungey
5 1/2 x 8 1/2, SC, 328 pp.
ISBN 0-88839-271-0 22.95

Puffin Cove:
A Queen Charlotte Islands Odyssey
Neil G. Carey
5 1/2 x 8 1/2, SC, 178 pp.
ISBN 0-88839-216-8 11.95

Yukoners
True Tales of the Yukon
Harry Gordon-Cooper
5 1/2 x 8 1/2, SC, 144 pp.
ISBN 0-88839-232-X 12.95

Nahanni
Dick Turner
5 1/2 x 8 1/2, SC, 286 pp.
ISBN 0-88839-028-9 11.95